Jack Kent

Jack Kent

The Wit, Whimsy, and Wisdom of a Comic Storyteller

PAUL V. ALLEN

University Press of Mississippi / Jackson

The University Press of Mississippi is the scholarly publishing agency of
the Mississippi Institutions of Higher Learning: Alcorn State University,
Delta State University, Jackson State University, Mississippi State University,
Mississippi University for Women, Mississippi Valley State University,
University of Mississippi, and University of Southern Mississippi.

www.upress.state.ms.us

The University Press of Mississippi is a member
of the Association of University Presses.

Copyright © 2023 by University Press of Mississippi
All rights reserved

First printing 2023

∞

Library of Congress Control Number: 2023008272

Hardback ISBN: 9781496846280
Trade paperback ISBN: 9781496846297
Epub single ISBN: 9781496846303
Epub institutional ISBN: 9781496846310
PDF single ISBN: 9781496846327
PDF institutional ISBN: 9781496846334

British Library Cataloging-in-Publication Data available

"It's fun to write a story.
Getting the idea is the hard thing.
But everything I ever did
or saw
or heard
or felt
has an idea in it.
So all I have to do is look about
inside my head.
In time, I find an idea to share with you."

— JACK KENT, "MEET JACK KENT" (1985)

Contents

Part 1

Chapter 1: From Pillar to Post (1920–1936) 3
Chapter 2: "Texas Jack" (1937–1941) 12
Chapter 3: Tedious Business (1942–1949) 17
Chapter 4: Willywampusses Are Chasing Geezles (1950) 23
Chapter 5: Love Is Ageless, Deathless . . . and Penniless
   (1951–1953) 29
Chapter 6: Junie and Jack Jr. (1953–1957) 39
Chapter 7: My Future Looks Rosy, but Not Very Big!
   (1957–1960) 49
Chapter 8: Illogical Conclusions (1960–1965) 57

Part 2

Chapter 9: From *Humpty Dumpty* to *Playboy* (1965–1968) 67
Chapter 10: The Sandbox Set (1968–1970) 76
Chapter 11: A Cartoonist at Heart (1971–1974) 87
Chapter 12: Fringe Benefits (1975–1979) 99
Chapter 13: No Great Genius (1980–1983) 108
Chapter 14: Just Only Jack (1984–1985) 118
Epilogue: Ever After (1986 and Beyond) 130

Acknowledgments 143
Appendix 144
Notes 158
References 166
Index 172

Part 1

Chapter 1

From Pillar to Post (1920–1936)

Jack Kent was born John Wellington Zurawski on 10 March 1920, the first child of Marguerite and Rudolf Zurawski. At that time the Zurawskis made their home in Burlington, Iowa, located on the Mississippi River and boasting a population at that time of about twenty-four thousand people. Marguerite and Rudolf had married just eleven months before their son's arrival.

Marguerite, usually called Peg, was a Burlington native, the youngest of six children born to Max and Mary Bruhl, both immigrants from Austria. Rudolf went by several nicknames: Ralph, Ray, Arthur, or just Art (the latter two after his middle name, Artur). His parents, John and Louisa (also called Louise), were both of Polish descent but had been born in Germany and West Prussia, respectively.

John Zurawski was a successful businessman, having immigrated at the age of eighteen and settled in Belle Plaine, Iowa. He worked his way through a few different jobs and cities, trading lumber in Remsen, banking in Le Mars and Dyersville, and finally becoming president of the Burlington Paper Company. The Zurawskis moved three times before Ralph was five, perhaps imprinting the wanderlust he'd be taken with in the middle of his life.

Like Peg, Ralph was the youngest of six. He was also—at least academically and professionally—the outlier of the family. His siblings were all college graduates with professional careers. Helen was at one time the head nurse at Johns Hopkins Hospital, Arnold served in World War I and became a dentist, Elizabeth and Florence were both teachers (Agnes died at the age of fifteen, when Ralph was just five).

Ralph, on the other hand, didn't attend college. When he married Peg, he was working as a stockman at his father's company.

By the time of Jack's arrival, Ralph had taken a job at Congoleum Company, selling commercial and residential flooring, including "Gold Seal" Congoleum, advertised as "durable, water-proof, and easy-to-clean."

The primary thing Jack's parents had in common was a shared sense of humor, and it was always at the ready. Peg was slight, a chain smoker with a fun-loving nature. Ralph was short and solidly built. He smoked cigars, drank heavily, and was a born storyteller, weaving hilarious yarns for whoever would listen. His gregarious nature served him well in sales.

For the first four years of Jack's life, the family remained rooted in Burlington while Ralph traveled. Early on, Jack showed a need to express himself through art. "Even before I could talk properly, I used to make 'kitty mows' on the wall," he revealed in a 1979 interview. "I think that meant, 'kittens saying meow.'" He was no prodigy—his kittens were little more than scribbles—but the desire to express himself in pictures was there very early on.

The Zurawski family grew by one in 1924 with the arrival of Mary Lou. That same year, Congoleum was purchased by New Jersey-based Nairn Linoleum, and the company became Congoleum Nairn. This seems to have expanded Ralph's sales opportunities, and he began to cover more territory. But rather than leave his young family at home when he traveled, Ralph started bringing them along. It's impossible to reconstruct the exact path the family took as they traveled, but there are definite landmarks. In the 1925 Iowa state census, they were listed as living in Davenport, Iowa, about an hour and a half north of Burlington.

Jack consistently said that he started school in Chicago, which is another 175 miles west of Davenport, but the Zurawskis weren't in the Windy City for long. This was because Ralph got a new position at Congoleum, becoming regional sales manager of the four-state block of Arkansas, Oklahoma, New Mexico, and Texas. It wasn't quite a plum assignment. Those four states were large and spread out in a time when there weren't a whole lot of paved roads or large cities. But Ralph's promotion resulted in two major developments.

For one, Ralph made the monumental decision to change the family name. He applied in November 1925 to legally change "Zurawski" to "Kent." On the form requesting the name change, Ralph claimed it would make his job as a salesman that much easier if he had a last name that was easy for customers to pronounce and remember. This was also a time when people of Polish heritage were subject to widespread stereotyping and discrimination, and that's surely something he had experienced firsthand.

The timing of the change was interesting, given that Ralph's father had passed away just the year before from heart failure while on a business trip (the *Sioux City Journal* reported it under the headline "Iowan Drops Dead in a Los Angeles Hotel"). Ralph clearly admired his father—choosing to name his son after him—and would always be proud of his Zurawski heritage, claiming a Polish count as an ancestor and prominently displaying the family crest—three gold hunting horns joined at the mouthpiece—wherever the family lived. Giving up the family name was clearly not something Ralph did lightly.

And why, specifically, did he choose "Kent"? This is a mystery. Ralph claimed in his application letter that his brother had taken the name before him, though there's no evidence of this (Arnold continued to use his family name until his death in 1954). The debut of Superman was still a few years away, but it's telling that Joe Shuster and Jerry Siegel dubbed their immigrant superhero Clark Kent; it was a name that was strong and memorable. While there were no ultrafamous Kents in 1925, there were a couple of notables who had that name, such as the painter, illustrator, and travel writer Rockwell Kent. Given Ralph's middle name (and childhood nickname), perhaps he took Kent from Arthur Kent, who owned the largest manufacturer of radios in the United States, Atwater Kent. Or maybe the Celtic and English origins of the name Kent were simply another example of the anglophile tendencies that also led Ralph and Peg to give their son the middle name of Wellington.

The Zurawskis officially became the Kents in 1926, and by that time, Ralph, Peg, Jack, and Mary Lou had landed in Houston, Texas. This, of course, was the second major development that resulted from Ralph's promotion. Why did they move so far south and not someplace like Dallas, which would have been much more central to

Jack and Mary Lou Kent in Seabrook, Texas, 1926. Courtesy of Jack Kent Jr.

Ralph's four-state area? Again, it's hard to know. Perhaps it's because the family had no intention of setting down roots.

Even with Jack in school, Peg and Ralph seemed to prefer a nomadic existence. As Ralph made his way around Texas, New Mexico, Oklahoma, and Arkansas, he took the family along. As Jack later put it, "Whenever we found a town we liked better than the one we lived in, we moved. I went to a different school every semester . . . sometimes two or three." As an adult he'd remember the names of some of the schools he attended—Austin, Chevy Chase, and Horace Mann—but not the cities in which they were located. Jack would say that he'd lived in every state in the union by age seventeen. This was an exaggeration, but it must have felt that way to young Jack.

Ralph and Peg thrived on motion and the promise of new places and fresh starts. Mary Lou would describe her parents as "the Twenties equivalent of hippies—pretty unconventional and fancy-free." Later, after they had both passed away, Mary Lou would make the intriguing remark that her parents had been "four-to-six of the most interesting people I've ever known."

The earliest surviving piece of art by Jack Kent, 1926. Jack Kent Jr. suggests this illustrates a familiar Kent family scenario, with Ralph saying, "no," but Peg saying, "yes." Courtesy of Jack Kent Jr.

Though neither had attended college, Ralph and Peg were both intelligent and well-read, transporting a good-sized library with them wherever they traveled. The elder Kents didn't always find lodgings for the family right away when they arrived in a new place, nor did they always have enough cash on hand to afford to eat. Sometimes they'd send Mary Lou and Jack to knock on doors and ask for food. Ralph and Peg were also adherents of Christian Science, in part believing that material things are an illusion, reality spiritual, and thus eschewing most medical treatments.

In general, Jack's parents discouraged their children from getting close to anyone outside of the family unit. That was essentially impossible anyway, as they rarely stayed in a place long enough to form any sort of meaningful friendships. As a result, Jack and Mary Lou relied on and supported one another. They'd also be very close with and protective of their parents for the rest of their lives.

Studies have found that frequent moves during childhood can have long-term negative effects on social and emotional development, especially if the moves involve changing schools. The latter is especially stressful and potentially harmful, triggering anxiety and impeding academic performance. And multiple childhood moves can have long-term effects. A 2010 longitudinal research study sponsored by the American Psychological Association found that adults who moved frequently as children reported lower "life satisfaction and psychological well-being" and an impaired ability to form and maintain relationships.

These negative effects were found to be more pronounced on those with introverted personalities, which Jack certainly had. Jack never talked much directly about how his childhood affected him, but it's clear that his personality, outlook on life, and decision-making would be heavily defined by his constant moves.

Though home, school, and friends weren't a consistent or reliable part of Jack's life, newspaper comics were. No doubt they both spoke to and fed his love of drawing. They were also something that remained constant no matter where he lived. Every city had newspapers and every newspaper had a comics page. The popularity of comic strips had grown wildly in the 1920s, and by the 1930s most papers devoted somewhere between twelve and twenty-four pages to them. Jack became obsessive about his favorite strips, clipping them, collecting them, studying them, and memorizing key information about them. He remembered, "When I was a boy I could have recited who drew what and when and for whom."

His favorite, or "my first great love," as Jack put it, was George Herriman's antic, surreal, poetic *Krazy Kat*, an ongoing tale of a love/hate triangle between a cat, a mouse, and a dog, which had started in newspapers two years before Jack's birth. Jack bought the *Chicago American* from his local newsstand expressly to read *Krazy Kat*, and on at least one occasion wrote the syndicate asking them to help him find Sunday strips he'd missed. Herriman became his model and idol and would remain so for the rest of Jack's life. In his final interview, Jack said of Herriman's impact on comic strips, "I think his work proves that the medium is an art."

Jack also particularly loved the *Little Orphan Annie*-inspired *Little Annie Rooney*, Tom McNamara's *Us Boys*, and E. C. Segar's *Thimble Theatre* (featuring Popeye). It wasn't long before Jack's life ambition was to have a comic strip of his own. His emerging and rapidly improving artistic talent made it seem like a real possibility.

• • •

The 1930 census found the Kent family living at 2011 Bissonet in Houston, just a couple of blocks from Rice University and a stone's throw from Chevy Chase Elementary School, where Jack attended. But by the next year the family had moved 200 miles west to San Antonio. Jack finished out his elementary school career at Highland Park Elementary School on Rigsby Avenue, moving on the next year to Thomas Nelson Page Junior High.

In 1934 the Kents moved to Dallas, where Jack started high school at Dal-Tec. Around this time Jack claimed to have sold his first cartoon, a one-panel gag to *Collier's Weekly*. Though it doesn't seem to have appeared in print—either the magazine bought it but didn't use it, or they allowed another cartoonist to execute Jack's idea—this was still a major accomplishment for a fourteen- or fifteen-year-old

The Kent family on a return visit to Burlington, Iowa, 1933. From left to right: Jack, Peg, Ralph, Mary Lou. Courtesy of Jack Kent Jr.

Caricature of realtor Arthur Baird Jack did for the *San Antonio Light* in the 1930s. Courtesy of Jack Kent Jr.

Caricature of furniture store owner Jake Karotkin Jack did for the *San Antonio Light* in the 1930s. Courtesy of Jack Kent Jr.

kid. In the 1930s *Collier's* regularly printed work by cartooning giants such as Charles Addams, William Steig, Barney Tobey, and Jay Irving. Though it would be many more years before he sold another cartoon, it's safe to say that this taste of professional success would shape the course of Jack's life significantly. For one, it gave him the confidence that he was on the right track. For another, it likely spurred a huge life decision he'd soon make.

As the effects of the Great Depression continued to spread, Ralph saw his flooring sales plummet, to the point that he decided to leave Congoleum Nairn. This meant yet another move, this time back to San Antonio, with the family taking up residence in the Acme Courts apartment complex on Route 7. Jack had the choice to either start over at yet another new school or to find a way to help his family financially. He chose the latter. He wouldn't enroll in high school in San Antonio to finish his final two years. "I gave it up" is how Jack would put it later.

And as unlikely as it sounds now to attempt to use cartooning to financially help out one's family, it was a viable path at the time.

Jack took a job as an apprentice in a print shop. He also occasionally created art for local advertising agencies. Ralph, meanwhile, landed a job at the Buckhorn Saloon in downtown, a bar/museum/tourist attraction known for its massive collection of antlers and mounted animal heads. Ralph—a prodigious drinker himself—found that his easy smile, loquaciousness, and extroversion served him well at the saloon. He eventually worked his way to becoming manager. Here he became known as "Tucky," which in the tenuous logic of nicknames may have been a play on his last name (Kent + Tucky = Kentucky).

In San Antonio for the second time, after over a decade of wandering, the Kents had finally found a forever home. Accordingly, sixteen-year-old Jack adopted a new persona. And like his father, he took on a new moniker to go with it. Mimicking the hearty, outgoing, confident spirit of his father, he began referring to himself as "Texas Jack."

Chapter 2

"Texas Jack" (1937–1941)

It's likely Jack had heard of the real Texas Jack, a man by the name of John Baker Omohundro, who was not a native Texan either, having been born and raised in Virginia. Omohundro got his nickname while working in Texas as a cowboy, then later served as a confederate soldier and a civilian scout during the American Indian Wars. After his military career, Omohundro became a stage actor in traveling Wild West shows along with the likes of "Buffalo Bill" Cody and "Wild Bill" Hickok. He wrote about his exploits in newspaper articles, and they became the subject of several dime novels in the late 1800s and early 1900s.

The creation of a myth around himself is surely what Jack was aiming for by dubbing himself the new Texas Jack. It was not a natural metamorphosis as much as an effort to define himself, an exploration of a new persona based on his father's gregarious man-about-town demeanor. Perhaps it was also out of necessity. Jack knew that if he were going to support the family and become a professional artist, he'd have to test the limits of his introverted nature. What better way than to play the role of a larger-than-life character?

To give further authenticity to this new identity, Jack designed his own cattle brand, a circle-bar-K that he actually registered with Bexar County. Not only that, but he also had an actual branding iron made. The *San Antonio Light* newspaper ran a story about it, featuring a picture of seventeen-year-old Jack and his iron. Perhaps he did fantasize about one day owning a ranch, but at present it was more about creating and furthering his image than anything else. It was self-promotion.

He also began to smoke a pipe. The story goes that, while he drew, Jack would chew on his pencil, which annoyed his father. Ralph said, "That looks stupid. You need to put a pipe in your mouth." So Jack got a pipe and began holding it in his mouth without lighting it. "That looks stupid," Ralph repeated, adding, "You need to light it." So Jack did, and it became not only part of being "Texas Jack" but a habit.

Finances stabilizing somewhat, the Kents moved out of Acme Courts and into a house at 506 Rigsby Avenue, a couple of blocks from where they'd lived just a few years earlier. In addition to his other work, Jack had begun doing caricatures of prominent locals for the *San Antonio Light*. These were inspired by the work of Miguel Covarrubias, whose heavily stylized and exaggerated portraits of famous people appeared in the likes of the *New Yorker* and *Vanity Fair*.

Jack continued to be crazy about comics, his obsession deepening as he got older. Part of this was the early 1930s arrival of adventure strips such as Alex Raymond's *Flash Gordon* and Milton Canniff's *Dickie Dare* and *Terry and the Pirates*. Jack followed them eagerly and had even begun corresponding with his cartoonist heroes. In 1937 it was exceedingly rare and difficult for amateurs in the arts to interact with professionals. In the case of cartoonists, one would have to write a letter to the artist in the care of the syndicate and then hope for a response. That's what Jack did. And, amazingly, it worked.

Among his first letters were some to Tom McNamara, whose strip *Us Boys* had run from 1912 through 1928. McNamara had worked on a couple of Sunday strips after that but by 1934 was doing screenwriting and making a transition to comic books. Jack's letters to the cartoonist were a combination of compliments, gentle probing, and breezy chitchat. He often included drawings, showing himself to be a gifted mimic of style and to already have a striking command of the visual language of cartooning.

McNamara wrote back and sent sketches, which no doubt fueled Jack's fire to write to more of his heroes. Milton Caniff appears to have been his next conquest, and Caniff also replied, sending preprinted character drawings and beginning a correspondence that led to Jack being included on the Caniff family Christmas card list for a time.

Jack contracted the measles in 1937, at that time a serious condition that often required hospitalization and could be fatal. His convalescence gave Jack the chance to contact more cartoonists, and he took advantage, amassing a collection of two hundred letters, sketches, photos, and original strips from the likes of Roy Crane, Chester Gould, Bob Lubbers, E. C. Segar, and Rube Goldberg. He typically signed his letters "Texas Jack" and included his circle-bar-K brand.

Though he'd never have formal art training, one could consider Jack's years of correspondence as a protracted internship. He got inside information about the ins and outs and ups and downs of his desired profession, and he received constructive feedback on his artwork. He'd later say, "I think the proper definition of self-taught is inspired or helped by so many people that the list is too long to recite."

On 31 October 1937, Jack made his very first appearance on the national newspaper page. Al Capp's wildly popular *Li'l Abner*, just three years into its 45-year run, regularly featured a section in the Sunday edition called "Advice fo' Chillin'," to which readers submitted bits of wisdom, which Capp then illustrated. Jack's, presented as a four-line rhyme, read:

"Li'l kid's [*sic*] what chews their nails, instead of bread and jelly—is apt as not to suffer a lot with sharp pains in their belly." It was credited to "Texas Jack" Kent, San Antonio, Texas.

• • •

Besides working and writing letters, Jack spent time buying books. Though he'd left school early, he had a deeply curious nature and a strong sense of wonder. Later he'd like to say that there was no topic that didn't interest him. Whether it was conscious or not, he began to take his abandoned education into his own hands. His collector's nature led him not to the public library but to local bookstores, where he began to build his own personal library. His favorite was Rosengren's Books, located in the Milam Building on Travis Street, just a few blocks from the Buckhorn Saloon.

Rosengren's was owned by Frank and Florence Rosengren, who had moved their store from Chicago to San Antonio sometime around 1935. Over time, the shop would become both a gathering place for bibliophiles and the center of the San Antonio literary community. The Rosengrens had some high profile nonlocal customers and friends, including Random House founder Bennett Cerf, poet Robert Frost, and *Madeline* author Ludwig Bemelmans. Teenage Jack became a regular at the store, befriending Frank and Florence and spending any cash he could spare on their stock.

In his eighteenth year, Jack's correspondence with cartoonists began to slow down, but he finally worked up the courage to write to his idol, George Herriman. Herriman had a reputation for generosity, so for his trouble Jack received a signed Sunday strip featuring "Lil Thin Dymme," which Herriman even had matted and framed. Jack would keep the strip hanging by his drawing desk for the rest of his days. Their correspondence continued, with Jack asking enthusiastically detailed questions about every aspect of Herriman's work and Herriman patiently responding. Some of Jack's questions were to fill in details about Herriman's other strips, some were about his work habits, and others were about the content of *Krazy Kat* itself. Jack later recalled, "There were frequent instances when the strip had a quotation or classic reference which was over my head. Herriman would explain it to me. I learned more from *Krazy Kat* than I ever did from school."

In 1938, Jack even endeavored to take a train ride to California to visit Herriman at his Hollywood home, but money trouble put the kibosh on the idea. The two did speak on the phone in 1940, and as part of the conversation Jack inquired about the *Krazy Kat* ballet, *Krazy Kat: A Jazz Pantomime*, that had been created in 1922 by composer John Alden Carpenter, but Herriman was unable to help Jack acquire a copy of the illustrated score.

His "Texas Jack" persona didn't just help Jack professionally. It also gave him confidence in other aspects of life, namely with girls. It didn't hurt that he'd grown into a handsome young man. To complement his blue eyes and brownish blonde hair, he began sporting a thin light-colored mustache he'd keep for the rest of his life. In 1938 he began seeing a fifteen-year-old girl named Odessa Seffel, a native of the nearby town of New Braunfels. How the two met is unknown, but Seffel was a coloratura soprano who sang live on the San Antonio radio station AM 1200, WOAI, and occasionally gave concerts, such as an April 1938 performance in the Crystal Room at the Aurora Apartments. Later that month, she performed in Houston for the Texas

State Teachers convention. Jack and Odessa's romance didn't last long, but she wouldn't be the last stage performer to catch Jack's eye.

• • •

The years 1939 and 1940 saw significant changes for the Kents. In 1939 Jack took a new job, becoming a staff artist at the Great American Life Insurance Company. Here, he created illustrations for both internal and external purposes, which was invaluable experience for a would-be cartoonist. The company was headquartered in a ten-story building on Pecan Street downtown, coincidentally not far from Rosengren's Books. The Kents also moved to a new house, this one at 323 Adams Street.

But the biggest development came in late 1940, when Jack took a gig as an art assistant to Elmer Woggon on the nationally syndicated strip *Big Chief Wahoo*. How he got the job is unknown, but it's likely that Woggon was one of the many cartoonists with whom Jack corresponded; he owned the original of a May 1939 *Big Chief Wahoo* strip. Geography was also to his advantage; the strip's artist, Elmer Woggon, lived in Houston. So Jack uprooted himself from San Antonio and headed east. At twenty-one years old, he was well on his way to his dream job. Working with Woggon gave Jack the chance to practice his craft at the professional level and to gain valuable insider experience in the mechanics of producing a daily strip.

Big Chief Wahoo, cocreated by Woggon and writer Allen Saunders, had begun in 1936 featuring a title character who was, in the words of author Mark Carlson-Ghost, "an embarrassing stereotype" of American Indians. In 1940, the feature would introduce photojournalist Steve Roper, who quickly overtook Wahoo as the main character. Wahoo disappeared completely from the strip in 1947. It eventually became *Steve Roper and Mike Nomad* and ran in newspapers for several decades.

But Jack was long gone from the strip before any of that happened. Like so many others in the United States, his life's course took a dramatic turn after the attack on Pearl Harbor on 7 December 1941. The United States was going to war, and so was Texas Jack.

Chapter 3

Tedious Business (1942–1949)

A matter of days after the attack on Pearl Harbor, Jack enlisted in the US Army. Some soldiers feel the urge to take care of unfinished business before leaving for basic training. One of Jack's primary goals was to finally meet his hero, George Herriman, in person. Sometime in either late 1941 or early 1942, he took a bus to Los Angeles and was able to spend a few hours with Herriman at his home. The elder cartoonist was in poor health, and Jack knew this was likely his only chance to tell his idol—face-to-face—just how much his work had meant to him. The pathologically modest Herriman didn't quite know how to handle the adulation. "I gushed and Herriman blushed," Jack said later.

But Herriman did dispense some advice. He told Jack that the most important thing he could do as a cartoonist was to be original. Jack said his time with Herriman sent him into an "ecstatic daze . . . a trance, a dream, from which I later awoke with the knowledge that something grand had happened." The two cartoonists continued to correspond, with Herriman sending Jack a hand-colored drawing in 1943 and wishing him luck in the second phase of his Army career: "Happy hunting 'Juanito' Git 'em before they start swarming over 'Santone'—Give 'em a touch of 'Alamo'".

Herriman wouldn't live to see the end of World War II. He died of liver failure in 1944 at the age of sixty-three.

After basic training, Jack was assigned to the field artillery and sent to Alaska. In June 1942, Japanese forces bombed two bases in the Aleutian Islands and occupied the islands of Attu and Kiska, located roughly fourteen hundred miles from the Alaska Peninsula. The United

The envelope that held George Herriman's note of encouragement to Private First Class Jack Kent, 1943. Courtesy of Jack Kent Jr.

States prioritized retaking the islands, largely out of fear that Japanese forces could use them as launching points for attacks on the US mainland. General Douglas MacArthur had anticipated the importance of the Aleutians, and in January 1941 sent the Army Signal Corps to start building a defense infrastructure, including a vast length of telephone wire system and the 1,420-mile Alaska-Canada Highway.

By the time Jack arrived with his unit, the main goal was the establishment of bases both in Alaska and on islands that could serve as refueling and maintenance stops, with the eventual goal of retaking Attu and Kiska. Jack served as what he described as a "code radio specialist," or what the Army called a "radio operator." This likely means that he was a signaler in charge of maintaining radio and telephone equipment and transmitting messages along the chain of command (sometimes in Morse code or encrypted code).

There were positives. Jack enjoyed seeing the northern lights and learning to cross-country ski (though it was less enjoyable when he had to do it in full battle gear). He also tried to learn to speak Eskimo, though it's hard to know which of the languages that fall under that umbrella term he actually studied. Jack would also be promoted to corporal during his time in Alaska.

Though officially he wasn't listed as having participated in any battles during his time in the Aleutians, Jack spoke of engaging in

Tedious Business (1942–1949)

hand-to-hand combat and told stories of rolling bombs out of cargo planes (before the Army Air Corps could send bombers). It took until May 1943 for the United States to retake Attu. It took another three months for the forces to attempt to take back Kiska, only to discover the Japanese had abandoned the island. After this, many of the Army and Navy bases in Alaska and the Aleutians were closed down.

Jack was sent back to the States, to Fort Sill in Oklahoma, where he became a candidate in field artillery officers' school, specializing in communication. It didn't go 100 percent smoothly, as Jack's free-thinking ways brought him to the brink of trouble. During an artillery training session, he missed his target and reoriented the gun based on the last position instead of returning to first principles. His commanding officer noticed this and said, "Okay, you can try that, but if you ever do it again I'll court-martial you." Jack fired the gun and hit the target dead on.

He also faced a challenge on his lieutenant's exam, which included a section on trigonometry. For most high school grads, this would just require a quick refresher, but Jack had left school before taking a class in trigonometry. And, when he'd enlisted, he'd lied about finishing high school. Jack's solution was to give himself an advanced mathematics crash course. He sequestered himself in the only lighted, quiet place on the base—the bathroom—and studied trig every night for a week. He passed the exam and became a lieutenant.

During the war, Peg Kent had taken a job as manager of the Maurer Apartments on Beauregard Street in the King William neighborhood, and she and Ralph moved into a two-bedroom apartment in the building. King William was an area of the city with a long history, full of historic old houses that had fallen on harder times and were now split up and rented by the room. Mary Lou was long gone, having married fellow San Antonian Dudley Cummins in 1940 and moved 150 miles west to Del Rio, on the Mexico border. While on leave from the Army, Jack stayed in the second bedroom, moving all of his belongings in there to make it a home.

Mary Lou and Dudley welcomed a son in 1943. They named him Kent, and he counts among his earliest memories visiting Ralph and Peg's apartment at the Maurer: eating Peg's special chocolate waffles, being shown the revolver Ralph kept on top of the refrigerator, and reverently looking around his Uncle Jack's room. He was fascinated by Jack's bunk bed, the posts of which were carved with Mexican designs. The wall facing the bed was a solid line of bookshelves. Jack's collection included several children's books, among them Ruth Krauss and Crockett Johnson's *The Carrot Seed* and Munro Leaf's *The Story of Ferdinand*, which Mary Lou would sometimes read aloud to Kent.

• • •

For the second half of his Army career, Jack was assigned to the 38th Infantry Division, also known as the Cyclone Division. They were deployed to the Pacific Theater in January 1944, initially to New Guinea, where they trained and saw limited combat. It was likely during this time that Jack, as he'd done in Alaska, began to study the native language. Tagalog is the first language of about a quarter of Filipinos and a second language to many others, and Jack worked to pick up basic vocabulary and phrases.

In December they moved on to the Philippine island of Leyte to aid in clearing and security. At the end of January 1945, they took part in the assault on the Japanese-held Zambales Province on the island of Luzon. More battles followed. Highway 7 in Luzon was nicknamed "Zig Zag Pass" and it was controlled by Japanese forces. To take it back, two regiments would attack, one from the front and one from the rear. The regiment coming from the back had to make a five-day march through mountains and junglelike terrain. The hard-fought battle lasted ten days and claimed heavy casualties on both sides before the US forces prevailed.

Next came a campaign to retake the Bataan peninsula, which had been captured by Japanese forces in April 1942. The defeat had resulted in 75,000 US and Filipino soldiers being forced to walk sixty-five miles to a prisoner-of-war camp under harsh conditions. Many didn't survive, leading the event to become known as the Bataan Death March. In a bloody battle, the Cyclone Division retook Bataan in February 1945. This, as well as subsequent successful efforts to secure Corregidor and Manila Bay, earned the division the nickname "the Avengers of Bataan."

Next, Jack volunteered to participate in the first phase of Operation Downfall, a multipart plan to invade the Japanese islands of Kyūshū and Honshu. The plan was anticipated to be analogous to the invasion of Normandy. Millions of Allied casualties were expected, and Jack was well aware that he only had a slim chance of returning home. The operation was slated to begin on 1 November 1945, but Japan surrendered following the atomic bombings of Hiroshima and Nagasaki in early August. The way Jack told it, he was on a troop ship to Japan when everyone was called up on deck and informed that the war was over and they were turning around. His division returned to the Philippines, where they helped with cleanup efforts.

On Halloween 1945, Jack landed back in the United States. His character and efficiency rating had been deemed excellent, and he was offered the chance to stay in the Army and become a career officer. "All due respect," he responded, "But I hate the Army and I'm leaving." His official final day in the military was 16 January 1946. He'd served for the entirety of the US involvement in World War II, and then some.

Jack's certificate of service indicated that he'd grown two inches since his enlistment, from 5'8" to 5'10". He was a lean 150 pounds. Though he came out of the Army taller and fitter, and had escaped major injury, Jack bore mental scars from his combat experiences. He was haunted by the deaths of his fellow soldiers and the deaths of Japanese soldiers by his own hand. He harbored a deep resentment at being trained to kill and having to carry that out. Though he rarely spoke of his war experiences, he once remarked, chillingly, "You can shoot a man until you swear there's nothing left of him and he's still coming to kill you." For the rest of his life, he was troubled by recurrent nightmares about his experiences in battle. He suffered from survivor's guilt and posttraumatic stress for the rest of his life.

• • •

Jack had briefly considered, upon landing in Los Angeles, staying in California and trying to land a job at Disney. But that wasn't his dream, and he had enough self-knowledge to know that his tendency toward insubordination wouldn't serve him well at a big company. So he returned to San Antonio. Like his fellow World War II servicemen, he was likely hailed as a hero, but otherwise he returned to a modest life. He moved fully into his room in his parents' apartment at the Maurer. Though he received twenty dollars a week for the first year following his discharge, he didn't laze about. He got a job at a printing plant. And though knowing how printing worked would be vital to his ambitions as a cartoonist, it must have felt like a significant step back from his prewar work on *Big Chief Wahoo*.

Thus would begin the second period of Jack's life in which he was forced to cobble together a living while still pushing forward with his ambition of becoming a syndicated cartoonist with his own strip. He described these times thusly: "If somebody had a job they needed done . . . they'd ask me, 'Do you do that?' My answer was always yes; I wasn't going to say no. Then I proceeded to do what I could with it."

Within a year of his return to San Antonio, Jack bought a parcel of land in the heart of the city. As the story goes, Ralph went out walking with young Kent to the nearby San Antonio River to "chase turtles and skip stones." While they made their way south along the river, Ralph noticed a vacant lot on Johnson Street. It had once been the site of a Victorian home that had been destroyed in the 1921 flood that caused five million dollars in damage and killed fifty-one San Antonians. Now it was an overgrown tangle dotted with pecan trees. The lot's owner had visions of using the land for a trailer park, but zoning laws forbade it. Ralph told his son about the land, and when Jack saw it himself, he decided to use his discharge pay to buy it. What exactly he was going to do with it he didn't yet know.

In addition to whatever paying work he was doing, Jack spent considerable time developing ideas for a comic strip he could submit to syndicates. One such idea was *Willy Nilly*, a Southwestern-set strip that featured an armadillo, rattlesnakes, and a bullfighting Mexican bird named Don Pilón. The strip was done in a European-inspired "ligne clair" style (so-called for the thin ink line, lack of rendering, and absence of black-white contrast) and displayed a love of puns (both in visuals and dialogue), dialects, and other languages. All of these presage what one presumes was Jack's next idea, the one that would help him, at the age of thirty, fulfill his lifelong ambition.

Chapter 4

Willywampusses Are Chasing Geezles (1950)

Jack sent *Willy Nilly* out to several syndicates, but none were interested in buying it. Jack went back to the drawing board, reasoning that if syndicates didn't want a sparsely drawn strip set in a real-world place, perhaps they'd want a lushly drawn strip set in an imaginary place. He invented a fairy tale kingdom overseen by a rotund little king and populated by a group of diverse and daffy subjects. This, Jack thought, just might be the perfect vehicle for the types of plots and jokes he wanted to tell, "with satire dancing antistrophe to the story."

The king would be kindhearted, if slightly dim. And of course he'd require an attendant. "Yupyop is the result of laziness on my part," Jack revealed in a 1955 interview. "A king needs a retinue and a one-man retinue takes less drawing than a full entourage." He'd admit, too, that he'd likely been subconsciously inspired by the character of Poo-Bah in Gilbert and Sullivan's comic opera *The Mikado*. Poo-Bah held several jobs at once, including "Lord High Everything Else."

With a twinkle in his eye, Jack named the tiny kingdom Myopia. The strip itself he called *Gizmo XXX*—a military jargon-inspired name that presumably doubled as the name of the king himself. In preparing samples for syndicates, Jack took his visual cues from a newish strip that was quickly gaining in popularity, Walt Kelly's *Pogo*. The strip had existed in comic book form since the early 1940s but became a nationally syndicated feature in May 1949. Kelly was a former Disney animator and had a richly detailed style built around expressive

23

character work and lovingly rendered backgrounds. *Pogo* featured a large cast of anthropomorphic animal characters and was a mélange of wordplay, songs, parody, and political satire.

Jack clearly took note of *Pogo* and its success and adjusted his style accordingly. He introduced a Kellyesque rendering into both his characters and his backgrounds and began using more black-and-white contrast. He even, unsurprisingly, struck up a correspondence with Walt Kelly himself. Kelly would build a reputation as someone who was, according to his wife Selby, "always trying to help somebody get a job." Accordingly, Kelly actually seems to have offered Jack a position as an assistant, likely to help with lettering and inking. Kelly already employed assistant George Ward (and would add Henry Shikuma in 1958). This is one of those crossroads moments we all get in our lives at various points. What if Jack had jumped at the chance for certain work on a strip that was on an ascent?

But Jack turned Kelly down. Unruffled, the *Pogo* cartoonist encouraged Jack to go to New York to drop off samples of *Gizmo XXX* to the syndicates in person. So, sometime in the first half of 1950, Jack took an 1,800-mile bus trip to New York to visit the major syndicates. Rarely did a prospective cartoonist talk to anyone with the power to make decisions, but presenting it to an actual person reduced the chances that the proposal would become lost in piles of mail. Jack included a note with his proposals that demonstrated his ability to take and learn from criticism: "I . . . would be forever grateful for a VERY BRIEF notation, on the back of a rejection slip, giving me some hint as to [the work's] PRINCIPAL fault, as you see it."

It wasn't long after he returned to Texas that Jack heard from the McClure Newspaper Syndicate. They loved his strip and wanted to offer him a contract. He was over the moon: "Willywampusses are chasing geezles up and down my spine and practicing handsprings in the pit of my stomach," he remarked.

McClure's only request was that Jack change the name of the strip. So *Gizmo XXX* became *King Aroo*. Where did the name come from? Jack never said, but it's likely there was no deep meaning and that it was simply a *Pogo*-esque play on "kangaroo." To further the confusion, King Aroo himself was a human, but one of the strip's main characters actually was a kangaroo, the mail carrier Mr. Pennipost.

Though *King Aroo*'s nonsensical title fit the tone of the strip, Jack may have inadvertently landed on something with deeper meaning. A persistent myth, not yet debunked in 1950, said that "kangaroo" was the native Aboriginal word for "I don't know." A king called "I don't know" is a perfect fit for a kingdom called Myopia. There's also the Ulustuk tribe of Native Americans in Maine, also known as the Aroostook, a name that in their language means "beautiful river" (and provides the name of a county in Maine, as well). Jack already owned land near the San Antonio river and would soon build his own tiny kingdom there.

McClure was not the most powerful or prestigious of newspaper syndicates in 1950, but it had a long-established history. In fact, it was the very first syndicate to be established, getting its start in 1884. In terms of comic strips, it had at one time been home to Rube Goldberg and Clare Victor Dwiggins (*School Days*). When *King Aroo* joined their offerings, McClure boasted Bob Montana's *Archie*, Carl Ryman's *Alfred*, Al Fagaly's *There Oughta Be a Law!*, and *Superman* (done at that time by Alvin Schwartz and Win Mortimer).

The comics page in general was undergoing a change in the early 1950s. In the late 1940s, the most popular comics were story strips that were at least fifteen years old: *Little Orphan Annie*, *Dick Tracy*, *Joe Palooka*, and *Li'l Abner*. However, the *most* successful newspaper comic in 1950 was Chic Young's *Blondie*, which had been around for twenty years but had moved away from melodrama to become a humorous, gag-a-day strip.

Indeed, as would quickly become clear, this was the trend of the 1950s. With strips like *Pogo* and Crockett Johnson's *Barnaby* leading the way, a whole new generation of cartoonists was emerging, and they would redefine the comics page. Within a seven-month period, the following strips debuted: Mort Walker's *Beetle Bailey* (4 Sep. 1950), Charles Schulz's *Peanuts* (2 Oct. 1950), and Hank Ketcham's *Dennis the Menace* (12 Mar. 1951). *King Aroo* was right in the middle of them, making its first appearance on 13 November 1950.

McClure placed *King Aroo* in the *New York Daily Mirror, San Francisco Chronicle, Houston Post, Chicago Tribune, St. Louis Globe Democrat, Kansas City Star*, and six major Canadian papers. A comic strip's popularity tended to grow by word of mouth, so starting in these major cities was a good launching point. An advertisement heralding the strip's arrival declared it to be "Fantastic! Whimsical! Wonderful!" and touted its appeal to children and adults alike. A brief article announcing the strip's arrival in the *Times Colonist* of Victoria, British Columbia, called *King Aroo* "pure fantasy and whimsey [*sic*]" and "one of the brightest newcomers in years."

Jack had tapped into the zeitgeist, just as the youngest children of the Baby Boom were reaching their storybook years. In March 1950 Disney had released its highly successful adaptation of *Cinderella*. Special effects master Ray Harryhausen was in the middle of creating and releasing stop-motion adaptations of fairy tales: "Little Red Riding Hood" (1949), "Hansel and Gretel" (1951), and "Rapunzel" (1951). Just a month after *King Aroo* appeared, James Thurber published *The 13 Clocks*, a self-aware, funny fairy tale that the Minneapolis *Star Tribune* called "childhood whimsy for grown-ups." Less than two years later the musical *Hans Christian Andersen*—a fairy tale imagining of the author's life—was a big hit in movie theaters.

The first three weeks of the *King Aroo* dailies allow a unique insight into Jack's presentation to syndicates, as it seems very likely that these were the very comics he included in his proposal. One big clue to this is the fact that the style is markedly different from the strips that follow. King Aroo and Yupyop are not quite in their final forms, both sporting smaller heads and bigger bodies than they'd later have. The settings are more solid and detailed than they'd ever be again, and, most interestingly, the Walt Kelly influence is actually less pronounced than it would be later (and in the Sunday strips that ran in Nov. 1950, which were clearly done after Jack signed his contract).

Story-wise it's easy to see what McClure saw in Jack's work. After a couple of introductory strips, he immediately dove into a plot in which Yupyop—practicing magical spells—accidentally turns a guinea pig into a moose (it's an accident because he was trying to turn the guinea pig into a mouse). Various antics ensue until a kiss from a lady moose breaks the spell. "Just like in a fairy story!" says King Aroo. It's fitting that his first storyline would be one about transformation, because that's a theme Jack would return to again and again in *King Aroo*, and long after that as well.

• • •

Once *King Aroo* got going, it became clear where Jack got his inspiration. Though *King Aroo* was much more than the sum of its parts, it had some definite antecedents. For one, it was indebted to *Krazy Kat* in its otherworldliness, sense of absurdity, incorporation of multiple languages, and occasional slapstick. Additionally, whenever Jack depicted a character throwing an object at another, he drew their throwing arm coming diagonally across their body, just the way Herriman drew Ignatz Mouse hurling a brick at Krazy.

Jack was also influenced heavily by *Pogo*, and the similarities between the two strips went beyond their visuals. Jack and Walt Kelly shared a love for the sounds of language (be they dialects of English or other languages completely), a tendency to lead their characters into mass misunderstandings, and an indulgence in metajokes (both cartoonists loved to have one character comment on another ones' awful pun). But there were differences too. Jack's characters were articulate but spoke more simply than Kelly's, and while both liked to play with language, Kelly bent more toward nonsense. As the two strips went on, *Pogo* would become more political and philosophical, while *King Aroo* remained largely whimsical and absurd, though both strips still occasionally crossed into one another's lanes.

Another influence on *King Aroo* was the comedy of vaudeville. Though the golden days of the comedy genre ended during Jack's childhood, its cultural impact endured in nearly all forms of mass entertainment, from radio (*The Abbott and Costello Show*) to movies (the Marx Brothers) to comic strips. *Little Nemo* cartoonist Winsor McKay was a regular on the vaudeville circuit, and Herriman, Rube Goldberg, E. C. Segar, and others embraced its antic absurdity (comics scholar Paul C. Tumey has grouped these comics into a subgenre he calls "screwball").

King Aroo fit snugly within that tradition. Jack imbued the strip with a spirit of improvisation, with jokes building upon one another until they all toppled over. Characters rarely correct one another, so misguided notions are escalated to absurd ends. In the 15 December 1950 strip, Yupyop sneaks into the castle to retake it from a lion. When the lion spots him, Yupyop pretends to be a clock using his fingers in front of his face and his right arm as a pendulum. He tells the lion it's eight o'clock and then proceeds to chime. The lion replies, without malice, "That's only seven!"

Finally, Jack's love of stories permeates *King Aroo*. It's no surprise, given the strip's premise, that fairy tales and fairy tale conventions show up regularly—in the first couple of months alone there are allusions to "Beauty and the Beast," "Cinderella," and the works of the Grimm Brothers and Hans Christian Andersen. References to nursery rhymes abound, and in fact the second storyline is set into motion by the first line of "Sing a Song of Sixpence" ("The king was in his counting house . . ."). But the literary allusions don't stop there, and Jack made clear the wide range of his reading with references in the strip's early days to everything from Lewis Carroll to the Bible, Izaak Walton to *Uncle Tom's Cabin*.

This combination of influences resulted in a comic strip that was simultaneously highbrow and lowbrow, parody and tribute. Take the Sunday, 24 December 1950 strip, in which a delegation of cats has come to visit. One of them says, "'A cat may look on a king,' as the saying is . . . but do we *have* to? I'd rather go to the zoo and look on the monkeys!" His companion responds, "Don't be bourgeois, Clarence!!"

Chapter 5

Love Is Ageless, Deathless . . . and Penniless (1951–1953)

At the age of thirty-one, Jack had achieved his professional dream. He was a nationally syndicated cartoonist. The hours required to keep up the pace of a daily strip were often impossibly long, but Jack had an unusually strong work ethic, and he clearly took great pleasure in creating adventures for his cast of Myopian misfits. One gets the idea that Jack always approached *King Aroo* with the idea of amusing himself first, his audience second.

For the first time in his life, Jack had a steady, significant income. So much so that Walt Kelly advised him in an early 1951 letter, "You better start counting your money." Jack's first order of business was to finally do something with the land he'd purchased on Johnson Street. He decided to design a house himself, spending about forty-five minutes sketching out a floor plan based on the layout of the Maurer apartment he still shared with his parents: two large living spaces with a bathroom and kitchen between them. It was simple, but the art of the place would be in its details. He imagined his new house as a "modernist homage to a Mexican hacienda." He gave it two terraces and arched stairs in the front and back that were inspired by ones in the Spanish Governor's Palace in downtown San Antonio. Instead of adobe, however, they'd be cast in concrete. Same with the walls. Instead of terra cotta Saltillo tile, the floors would be structural clay tile. The windows would be industrial aluminum instead of wood.

He hired contractor Joe Rivero to figure out the practical aspects. The pair even took a road trip to Mexico to pick out ceramic Talavera tile for the bathroom and kitchen, stopping at a few bars along the way. Measuring 18-feet wide and 75-feet long, the house looked so large upon construction that neighbors asked if a warehouse was going up.

A 1952 postcard of the house describes it thusly: "An unusual Spanish influence, ranch style home, showing semi-tropical plants which thrive in San Antonio's mild climate. This is just one of the many unusual homes to be found in cosmopolitan San Antonio, Texas. Designed by Jack Kent, creator of the internationally famous comic strip 'King Aroo.'" This was accompanied by Jack's depictions of the Alamo, King Aroo, and a bull.

Once the house was finished, the Kents all moved in, with Ralph and Peg taking the smaller front room as a bedroom and living room, and Jack using the larger room for a bedroom and studio. Jack also outfitted the house with an oversized mailbox, likely to accommodate his original artwork traveling back and forth to New York. He even added a primitive alarm system on the box so that only he and the mail carrier had access to it.

Jack's next big splurge was a used baby grand piano, which he bought at Alamo Music. He'd also finally tracked down a copy of the elusive *Krazy Kat: A Jazz Pantomime* sheet music and set about teaching himself to play it.

Jack traveled to New York semiregularly in the early days of *King Aroo*, now able to fly instead of enduring a days-long bus ride. These trips were for business, but Jack always worked in a bit of pleasure, too. He formed a group of friends that included fellow cartoonists and artists, many met through the National Cartoonist's Society, of which Jack was now a member. In his visits to the big city he'd also made the acquaintance of a singer and actress named Leigh Allen, who at that time was playing Ensign Lisa Minelli in the hit Broadway production *South Pacific*. Leigh, a soprano (like Odessa Seffel before her), was "a slender, picturesque blonde with blue eyes" and a native of the Bay Area in California. Prior to *South Pacific*, Leigh had appeared in touring productions of *Brigadoon* and *Great to Be Alive!*

Leigh captured Jack's heart. Walter Winchell picked up on the story in June 1951 for his gossip column "Winchell on Broadway," which appeared in newspapers nationally. According to Winchell, Jack sent Leigh a neatly boxed red rose every day, timed to arrive backstage right before curtain.

But even that wasn't enough to woo Leigh, so Jack used three separate *King Aroo* Sunday strips to broadcast his feelings. In the first, published on 24 June 1951, Yupyop sees Leigh—portrayed as the handmaiden of the Beautiful Princess from the kingdom next door to Myopia—and is smitten. The next week, he pines over her and gets angry when King Aroo scrawls "Yupyop loves Leigh" on the castle wall. Then, two weeks later in the 22 July strip, King Aroo gives an update: "He's serious, she considers him a 'good friend.'" But then Yupyop reveals Leigh has finally agreed to a dinner date and spends the rest of the strip getting ready by retrieving his toupee from some birds who were using it for a nest. This would be the final mention of Yupyop's affair with Leigh, which is a strong indication that the dinner date between Jack and the real Leigh did not go well.

. . .

Largely escaping the awkward phase most ongoing comic strips go through in their early days, *King Aroo* settled into itself quickly. It hummed along through its first anniversary as Jack gradually introduced his cast of characters. There was Mr. Pennipost, who uses his pouch to hold letters and packages (Jack was well aware that male kangaroos don't have pouches, relishing the absurdity of it). Mr. Elephant has a memory so bad he can't remember what he was trying to remember. Professor Yorgle is extensively educated but is still quite unable to prevent everyone else from chasing their misguided notions. And Wanda Witch casts her spells by literally throwing bottles of potions. Providing support to these main players was an ever-expanding roster of mostly animal characters.

The parameters of the strip also developed quickly. Myopia is perpetually in financial trouble (their only income is from the rent paid by a frog to live in the castle's moat) but never that worried about it.

32 Love Is Ageless, Deathless . . . and Penniless (1951–1953)

Its newspaper, the *Myopia Gazette*, only has one subscriber (the king himself). The kingdom has a train station but no railroad to go with it.

Structurally, Jack tended to tell a two- or three-week ongoing story in the dailies, while the Sunday strips stood alone narratively (though occasionally following a theme for a couple of weeks in a row). In 1951, the strip raced through storylines, including a memorable April sequence in which the cast confuses a balloon for the moon and a November episode in which Professor Yorgle is accidentally transformed into a seal and must learn more about his new self by reading *The Care and Feeding of Seals*.

By the time the calendar turned over to 1952, everything about *King Aroo*—Jack's cartooning, the characters, the storytelling—was working in harmonious tandem.

One of the qualities that made *King Aroo* stand out on the comics page was the way it played with language. Jack's fascination with funny-sounding words—rutabaga, kumquat, doodlebugs, boll weevils, nuthatches, tutti-frutti ice cream, and Spindly Thicket (a place often mentioned but never seen)—ran throughout the strip. Wordplay was the basis of a large percentage of *King Aroo*'s jokes, showing up in puns, takeoffs on idioms, and the parade of animals—both real and invented—who take their names literally. And Jack's interest in other languages led him to utilize foreign words and phrases often.

Puns were a bedrock of Jack's sense of humor. He seemed to recognize that puns can typically be divided into three categories—clever, groan-worthy, and bad—and didn't limit himself to just one kind. On the clever side, there's the 1954 exchange in which Max Mockingbird imitates a star. "Twinkle! Twinkle! Twinkle!" he says. "Is he serious, Yupyop?!" Mrs. Mooley asks. Yupyop replies, "I wouldn't know—I can't tell Sirius from Betelgeuse. . . ."

On the groaner side are jokes like Yupyop's magician's patter from a January 1951 strip: "You'll note that this hat is bald. . . . but I'm going to remove a hare from it." Or when the Ibex reveals, "I've got acrophobia so bad I couldn't even go to high school."

If a pun was especially bad that didn't stop Jack from using it, but he typically had a character comment on it. After a bad one about Drexel Dragon's tail "a-draggin'," Yupyop reacts angrily: "Puns! Puns! Puns! All my life I've had to put up with such cheap wit!" In an April

1962 strip King Aroo acknowledges a bad pun about his nose running, remarking, "Sometimes when I'm obliged to deliver a line like that, I wonder if it's all really worthwhile."

Just as often *King Aroo*'s humor came from characters mistaking the figurative for the literal, or, by the rules of fantasy, the figurative actually being literal. The weather bureau in Myopia is an actual bureau of drawers, with different types of weather in each drawer. You can probably guess what the missing persons bureau is, as well. Sarah the Siren (a pelican who tries to wreck ships) reveals that her sister is a fire siren, though she served as an air raid siren during the war. Ben the Bull wants to open a china shop but is instead encouraged to work in the stock market. There's also the Millionairedale, of whom it's told "poverty dogged his footsteps" before he struck it rich. A weasel goes around saying, "Pop!" It goes on and on.

And then there was Jack's fascination with foreign languages. Perhaps most prominently, Jack utilized some Tagalog phrases he'd learned in the Philippines during the war. A short article in *Newsweek* pointed out that one of the spells Wanda Witch incants ("halika, multo, madali, madali") in a 1 June 1952 Sunday strip was not nonsense but actually Tagalog for "come here, ghost, quickly, quickly." The article stated that Jack went so far as to check his work with the National Language Institute of the Philippines before publishing. He did it again in a 1956 strip in which Wanda says, "Kumasta po kayo ning" ("How are you doing?").

In a very early strip, Yupyop's magic words come from various American Indian tribal languages—Cheektowaga! Lackawanna! Canajoharie! Oswego!"—and also happen to be the names of places in New York and Pennsylvania that Jack may have noticed on his bus rides. Many other languages would make regular appearances in *King Aroo*: German, French, Greek, Chinese, Dutch, and even Egyptian hieroglyphics. An early 1952 storyline concerns a camel who speaks only Arabic (Jack clearly had fun writing in the calligraphy of the language). He loved using Latin, especially in giving the Latin names of various species (typically accurate, but sometimes invented, as with the Synopsis bird, Rerum Repetitio of the genus Summarium). And, in line with Jack's love with Mexican culture, Spanish also recurred frequently, often as part of casual conversation.

• • •

At some point, likely after his doomed dinner date with Leigh Allen, Jack fell for another blonde, a highly driven 34-year-old Jill-of-all-trades named Juliet Bridgman. She called Jack to inquire about the film rights to *King Aroo*. The two met, and Juliet became Jack's agent. Her primary goal was to bring *King Aroo* to television, but she was also on the lookout for other marketing and licensing opportunities for the strip and its characters.

Like Jack, Juliet had spent much of her childhood moving from place to place. Her inventor/entrepreneur father Harry had separated from her mother Margaret—a German-born astrologer, writer, and lecturer—when Juliet was young. Margaret had little interest in being a mother, so she sent Juliet and her older brother Henry to boarding schools and a foster home in Staten Island. When Juliet was around nine years old, Harry Bridgman fell ill and decided to take belated responsibility for his children. Two years later, Harry died while he and the children were living in Los Angeles.

Harry and Juliet took a train across the country back to New York, and Margaret promptly sent Juliet to live with her grandmother in Berlin. In Berlin she trained with a Russian ballerina at an academy in the city, but her grandmother died when she was sixteen, leaving Juliet essentially on her own. She went to Paris, where she became a dancer in the Cabaret Bergère and found work as a scriptwriter and commentator for a Paris radio station. She then moved on to Italy, where she worked as a dancer, actress, and model.

Also like Jack, Juliet was largely an autodidact; her tumultuous early life meant her formal schooling was spotty, and she didn't pursue higher education because she couldn't afford it. But she had a facility for languages. In addition to being fluent in German, she would eventually pick up a working knowledge of Spanish, French, Italian, Portuguese, and Russian.

In 1940, 22-year-old Juliet returned to the United States and began a career as a freelance journalist, placing articles in the likes of *Esquire* and *Liberty* magazines. After the German surrender in 1945, *New York Magazine* sent her to East Berlin, and there Juliet's familiarity with the Russian language allowed her to arrange exclusive interviews with Russian officers. Upon returning home, she took a job as a performer, interpreter, and writer for the Ringling Brothers and Barnum and

Juliet Bridgman ca. the mid-1950s. Courtesy of Craig Bridgman.

Bailey Circus. She rode elephants in the show but also documented the lives and work of her fellow performers, often placing articles about the circus in the *Saturday Evening Post* and the *This Week* Sunday magazine supplement.

In 1951 she wrote an episode of the CBS murder mystery anthology series *Danger*. The episode, directed by Sidney Lumet, was called "The Killer Scarf," and it featured not only Anne Bancroft but also four joeys from the circus. Perhaps this taste of television success is what inspired a desire to branch out to producing. Juliet managed to land *King Aroo* at New York-based Fletcher Smith Studios, who created a pilot reel and began shopping it around for distribution.

As this was going on, Jack and Juliet fell in love. In addition to being drawn in by her "glamorous" good looks and husky voice, Jack was attracted to the fact that Juliet was ambitious and intelligent. In turn, he charmed her with his Texas gentleman persona—wearing his cowboy boots and hat even on trips to New York—and with acts of kindness and generosity, such as presenting her nephew Craig with a Christmas gift of a pair of handmade, hand-tooled cowboy boots he'd long wished for. He also gave Craig's family an original drawing to help inaugurate the bathroom of the house they were building in the Pocono Mountains. It featured Yupyop standing next to a newly installed toilet and calling out, "The throne is ready for the royal flush, King Aroo!"

After a brief courtship, Jack proposed, Juliet accepted, and the two were married at New York's Little Church Around the Corner on 27 September 1952. It's not known whether they took a honeymoon trip, but a couple of weeks after their wedding, the couple were in Chicago visiting Tribune Tower to celebrate *King Aroo* getting picked up by the Chicago Tribune-New York News syndicate. This added the strip to an additional thirty papers with a circulation of thirty million (including papers in Sweden and the Philippines). The strip also began appearing in French in Quebec, where it was known as *Le Roi Zozo*, a name which tickled Jack greatly.

With a possible TV series, Jack in the midst of working out a book deal for *King Aroo*, and much of Juliet's business and life taking place in New York, it would have made sense for Jack to relocate there. But instead it was decided that they would make their home in San Antonio. One assumes that there were a couple of factors at play here. The largest was likely that Jack had already invested a lot—both financially and emotionally—in the house on Johnson Street. In fact, he had insisted on a clause in his McClure contract that he not have to move to New York. The other factor may have simply been that, after his itinerant childhood and far-flung stint in the Army, Jack didn't want to have to get settled, yet again, in an entirely new place. On top of all of that, he genuinely loved San Antonio.

Jack and Juliet's marriage was doomed nearly from the start, though there are conflicting stories about exactly when and how they discovered it wouldn't work. There's at least some indication that Juliet did try to settle in San Antonio, with Juliet having not only to adjust to being newly married and living in a whole different part of the country but also to sharing a house with Jack's parents. Juliet would later tell her family that the couple had never lived together, because she'd realized the marriage was a mistake before they ever settled in San Antonio.

No matter the exact details, it seems that passion had blinded Jack and Juliet to at least three major obstacles to spending the rest of their lives together. One was that Juliet didn't want to settle in Texas. Another was that she had no interest in being a mother, even though Jack definitely wanted to start a family, and soon. And the third was the fact that, although Jack and Juliet had a lot in common, their professional trajectories didn't match. Juliet was someone who was constantly on the go, with an abiding love of travel and adventure. Jack loved to travel too, but producing a daily strip meant he was constantly on a deadline. He was effectively chained to his drawing table. In a 1985 interview, he reflected on this time, "If you do, as I did, the whole thing yourself, with no studio, no assistance—if you are too selfish to share the fun—you were working fifteen to eighteen hours a day, seven days a week."

Jack and Juliet divorced in May 1953 after only eight months as husband and wife. Juliet headed back East, where she continued to work in promotion and public relations, eventually opening her own firm. In the late 1950s, she was assigned by an airline to go along on a South American fishing tour, and she fell in love with the experience. In the early 1960s, she began organizing and leading her own fishing and hunting expeditions in Argentina, through a company she called Bridgman Tours. This was highly successful and lucrative, and even led to her being featured in a 1962 episode of the CBS game show *To Tell the Truth* in which panelists tried to guess which of three contests was lying about their occupation or an experience they'd had.

In a newspaper article around that time, Juliet was described as a "confirmed bachelor girl" and seemed to erase her marriage to Jack from her history. She told the reporter, "Look, if I ever accepted a proposal I'd never be able to go off on a fishing junket again. And that's a fate worse than death."

For his part, Jack was truly heartbroken by his failed marriage but didn't hold any great anger or animosity toward Juliet. He wrote a letter to her after the divorce, expressing his deep sadness but remaining respectful and understanding. At some point during their brief marriage, Jack and Juliet got news that the networks had passed on the *King Aroo* pilot. This must have been a big disappointment and couldn't have helped their relationship. One bit of success Juliet did have was using her connections to license *King Aroo* to the Ringling Brothers and Barnum and Bailey Circus. So 1953 circus-goers were treated to life-sized King Aroo and Mr. Pennipost marching in the grand parade.

After his embarrassing experience with expressing his ardor for Leigh Allen in *King Aroo*, Jack seemingly became reluctant to mix his romantic life with his cartooning life, so Juliet was never mentioned in the comic strip. A February 1953 *People Today* article profiling Jack and Juliet claimed she was the model for *King Aroo*'s Beautiful Princess. And while she couldn't have been the inspiration for the character (the Beautiful Princess appeared in the strip before Jack met Juliet), it may very well be true that once they met he began to pattern the character after Juliet. It's fitting then, that King Aroo's relationship with the Beautiful Princess never really goes anywhere. In a series of strips from April 1963—which marks the character's last appearance—the Beautiful Princess and her retinue come to stay at the castle, but she ends up driving everyone out (she makes King Aroo and Yupyop clean; she hits the castle mice with a broom). She then leaves, saying, "We're going home! Your castle is too lonely."

Despite the failure of his relationship with Juliet, Jack didn't lose his yen for romance or his desire to settle down and start a family. Not long after his divorce was finalized, he asked Camille, the daughter-in-law of Frank and Florence Rosengren, what he could do to make a good impression on eligible women. Camille, instead of saying something philosophical like "be yourself" or "project confidence," told Jack that women like a man who drives a nice car. So Jack headed to the dealership and bought a brand new Lincoln Capri convertible right off the showroom floor. It was such an impulsive decision that he'd forgotten he didn't have a driver's license. The salesman agreed to drive Jack to the Department of Public Services as part of the deal.

Chapter 6

Junie and Jack Jr. (1953–1957)

In March 1953, as his marriage to Juliet was ending, Jack's first book—a collection of *King Aroo* strips—was published. This was a great opportunity to increase the strip's profile. Not only would it expose it to a larger audience, but it had the potential to expand the number of papers that carried the strip. *Pogo* books had started appearing in stores in 1951 and helped push that strip's popularity. The first *Peanuts* collection came out in 1952, and its books would prove to be a big factor in the strip's journey to ubiquity.

The *King Aroo* book—ironically, given the timing, dedicated to Juliet—was a collection of thirteen episodes from 1950, 1951, and 1952. Like the *Pogo* books, they were not presented as strips, but in comic book form with six panels per page. This had the effect of emphasizing the overall storyline over the daily joke. The collection came with a three and a half–page introduction written by Gilbert Seldes, an author, editor, and cultural critic. Seldes was known for his 1924 book *The Seven Lively Arts*, in which he defended such "lowbrow" forms of entertainment as musical comedy, newspaper columns, popular songs, vaudeville, and, yes, comic strips. He argued that these art forms had just as much potential validity as "highbrow" arts such as classical music, opera, novels, and painting. Included in his book was an essay titled "The Krazy Kat That Walks by Himself," a celebration and analysis of George Herriman's work.

Given Jack's love of *Krazy Kat*, it was both fitting and significant that Seldes also wrote about *King Aroo*. He was highly praiseful, singling out the fact that Jack's plotting in the strip was satisfying on

39

a daily basis but richer in the continuing stories. Seldes was also impressed with *King Aroo*'s conceit, writing, "Jack Kent belongs to the small company of fantasists [with] the primary faculty of being able to create a compact universe that adheres strictly to a logic of its own." He added, "Kent makes the best of two worlds, with warmth in his parodies, with sudden flashes of common-sense reality, and with genuine appreciation of the validity of all true mythologies."

Seldes was amazed that Jack had not finished high school. "His exuberance of language, the quirks in his vocabulary, are as specific marks of imagination as the constantly curving line he favors for the drawing of his small round characters."

Several newspapers published glowing reviews of the *King Aroo* collection, and Jack was featured in a late February *People Today*, a pocket-sized men's magazine with Doris Day on the cover and King Aroo on the back. The article gave a brief summary of Jack's success story and included a posed picture of Jack and Juliet. Besides that, however, no other national publications appear to have written about the *King Aroo* collection. Sales don't appear to have been particularly wonderful. The biggest indicator of that is the fact that there was no follow-up collection.

Complicating matters on that front was the fact that in September 1952 McClure was acquired by the Bell Syndicate-North American Newspaper Alliance. Bell had a number of successful comic strips in their stable in the 1920s and 1940s, but by the 1950s had a very small number of comic page "hits," limited mainly to the puzzle feature *Uncle Art's Funland* and George Baker's *Sad Sack*. So the merger came at an inopportune time for *King Aroo*, as Bell wasn't in a great position to grow the strip right at the moment when it was most crucial to do so. With the failure of the TV show and the book's sales stalling, increasing *King Aroo*'s circulation was the only hope for its long-term survival, and Jack's financial fortunes.

Even at its height, *King Aroo* never ran in more than one hundred papers. This meant it reached tens of millions of readers, but it wasn't a hit by comic strip standards. By contrast, consider Jack's contemporaries. Of the strips that had started at the same time—*Beetle Bailey*, *Peanuts*, and *Dennis the Menace*—only the latter had been a fast grower, reaching one hundred papers by the end of its first year,

Jack at home in the mid-1950s. Courtesy of Jack Kent Jr.

nearly two hundred in 1953. *Beetle Bailey* was almost canceled after getting only twenty-five newspapers during its first year, but by 1953 was in over two hundred, and Mort Walker was awarded the "outstanding cartoonist of the year" Ruben Award. *Peanuts* had debuted in only seven papers (two of which dropped it in the first year) but steadily grew each subsequent year and, by 1953, was beginning to show exponential growth. All three would eventually be in well over one thousand newspapers.

By the end of 1953, *King Aroo* was showing no such signs of growth and would settle firmly in the territory of a well-respected but not widely known "cult favorite." This was yet another way in which Jack had followed in the footsteps of his idol, George Herriman. For all its acclaim and influence, *Krazy Kat* was never massively popular; it endured because publisher William Randolph Hearst was a fan, and he kept the strip alive in his papers. Jack claimed that Gilbert Seldes once told him, "I've never seen admiration carried so far. You WRITE like Herriman." Jack added wryly, "It was a warning."

It's ironic in many ways that 1953 marked a downward turn in *King Aroo*'s fortunes. For one thing, it was the addition of the strip to a newspaper that led to the most significant development of Jack's life so far—but we'll get to that in a bit. The year 1953 was also, in terms of story and humor, perhaps the strip's most memorable and bravura year. It was a year in which King Aroo and Yupyop took multiple journeys: to London, to a new land called Hebefrenia, and through the grandfather clock into "yesterday's dumping ground," Langsyne. King Aroo even started the year by orbiting the Earth in Ben Abou Riley's flying carpet bag. In these storylines the strip is at its most literate, layered, and lighthearted.

In early *King Aroo* promotional materials, Jack's syndicate compared him to "an American Lewis Carroll." While that may have been hyperbolic, Jack definitely took some of his sensibility from *Alice's Adventures in Wonderland* and *Through the Looking-Glass*, especially in his use of nonsensical situations and "we're all mad here" characters. And Jack had even alluded directly to Carroll's work in an August 1951 strip where Mr. Walrus—who's looking at renting the moat—introduces his friend Joe the Carpenter Bird. This, of course, was a tribute to Carroll's "The Walrus and the Carpenter" from *Through the Looking-Glass*.

Jack and Carroll both traded freely in misunderstandings between characters and between characters and the world around them. While on her first journey through Wonderland, Alice begins to have an identity crisis. Likewise, in *King Aroo*, the characters' misguided notions come from a lack of self-knowledge or a loss of their identity.

The 25 April 1953 strip is a perfect example of the Carroll-worthy levels of absurdity Jack piled on. As King Aroo and Professor Yorgle are walking together, the king remarks that he's happy that spring has arrived because it means he can have his bed back. Professor Yorgle is understandably confused, until the king reveals that Mr. Elephant has been using it to hibernate. When Professor Yorgle points out that elephants don't hibernate, King Aroo says that Mr. Elephant is under the impression that he's a giraffe. "But King Aroo," Yorgle says, "giraffes don't hibernate either!" The king responds, "Then I've been sleeping in the bathtub all winter for nothing?!?!"

In an October 1953 strip, *King Aroo* tries to give a tour of his castle to a visiting tourist, but when he knocks on the door and doesn't get an answer, he says, "I guess we'll have to come back later—I don't seem to be home just now."

Again and again King Aroo's characters come to the wrong conclusions, and not just about themselves. Characters also have a tendency to misinterpret the world around them, especially as it pertains to matters of science. Perhaps this is because of an inherently magical place like Myopia trying to reconcile the findings of scientific research. In a 1953 Sunday strip, Yupyop and King Aroo believe that because the Earth is spinning that means they'll soon arrive in the kingdom next door. Yorgle's attempts to explain and clarify just further confuse matters. "In just a little while, West Myopia will be here . . . but, by then, we'll be somewhere east of here and . . ." King Aroo interrupts, "If we aren't going to be home, we'd better leave a note."

Perhaps the most Carroll-esque of all the *King Aroo* storylines is the summer 1953 sequence in which King Aroo and Yupyop visit a new land called Hebefrenia. True to its name— hebephrenia is a disorganized form of schizophrenia characterized by incoherent delusions—this is a kingdom where whatever you imagine comes true. After meeting a diminutive resident who instructs them on the way things work in Hebefrenia, they briefly attend school, where the teacher, who looks like a child's chalkboard caricature of a teacher, takes the role of the Mad Hatter. She's more interested in telling jokes and riddles than imparting knowledge. Of course, she's also full of misinformation. When she mentions Sir Isaac Walton falling into a vat of applesauce, Yupyop says, "I thought it was Newton." Her reply: "No—I'm positive it was applesauce."

The sequence goes on with a visit to three judges who "never do anything 'til after we've made a law against it," and then they move on to meet the king of Hebefrenia. The king ends up selling his crown to Aroo, effectively transferring power. And thus Hebefrenia ends up becoming incorporated into Myopia. For a while after this storyline, Hebefrenia's distinctive columns and sculptural figments of imagination can be seen in *King Aroo*'s background landscapes.

• • •

Now to that significant development. In August 1953 one of Jack's hometown newspapers—the *San Antonio Express and News*—finally began to run *King Aroo*. To mark the occasion, the paper sent a reporter to interview the city's semifamous son at home. The reporter's name was June Kilstofte, and she had worked for the *Express* since the end of World War II. In 1952 she'd become editor of the *Express* Sunday magazine.

June's article, titled "King Aroo's Castle," appeared in that Sunday magazine in October 1953. In the article, she outlined Jack's journey and seemed quite taken with his home. She detailed the lawn lined with pecan trees and the feeling of being in the country right in the middle of the city. Included in the profile were pictures of Peg Kent in the kitchen preparing muffins and a pipe-smoking Jack sitting in his studio/bedroom in front of his bookshelves.

"There's a special shelf for foreign language dictionaries," June noted.

As for Jack, June found him to be "a very friendly guy." Some of that friendliness was surely due to the fact that Jack found his interviewer to be quite attractive. She was tall and slim, with dark hair that she wore up, a slightly upturned nose, and a wide smile that brought out two large dimples on either side. As they were touring the house, Jack pointed out that during the winter he'd regularly place birdseed on his windowsill. Once spring arrived he stopped doing it, but a bird still kept showing up, saying, "Cheap, cheap!" June laughed at the bad pun, and Jack took it as an opening to ask her out on a date. She said yes.

Jack had a type. Like Juliet before her, June was a writer who was independent, accomplished, and fiercely intelligent. Born in Chicago on 9 June 1920 (making her just three months younger than Jack), June spent her early years in Chicago, where her grandfather, Peder Kilstofte, was a successful building contractor and her father, Holger, worked as brick mason. Her mother, Kate, and older brother, Howard, rounded out the family.

When the Great Depression hit, Peder's business went under, so June's family headed first to Minneapolis and then settled at Peder's farm in Askov, Minnesota, a small town about sixty miles southwest of Duluth. Peder and June's grandmother, Marie, were both immigrants from Denmark, as was Kate Kilstofte, so Askov—with its strong Danish cultural heritage—was a good fit for the family. Here June attended middle school and high school, graduating as valedictorian of her class at Askov High School. The school's nickname was "The Danes." (Askov was and is known for its annual Rutabaga Festival and Fair, a fact that—given his obsession with that particular vegetable's name—surely tickled Jack).

For college, June chose to return to Minneapolis and attend the University of Minnesota. She'd dreamed of becoming an architect, but the program was too expensive, so she settled for a major in journalism. Though it was a second choice, she put her all into it, joining and becoming highly involved in the Theta Sigma Phi journalism sorority.

Holger, who went by the nickname Happy, had continued to work as a mason. While June was still in college, Kilstofte & Company won a bid to build the Lincoln Heights Courts, a housing project on the west side of San Antonio. Happy and his brothers moved to Texas to oversee the project, while Kate stayed behind with June so she could finish college. When June graduated in 1942, she and her mother followed the family south.

For a while after graduation, June kept the books for Kilstofte & Company, but eventually she moved on to a position at the public information office at Fort Sam Houston. In her free time she became involved with a group of female airplane pilots called the Women Flyers. She even served as secretary for the organization for a spell but had to keep her involvement a secret from her mother, who disapproved. After a crash in which she was lucky to walk away with only a cut on her chin, June's time with the Flyers was over.

While working at the *San Antonio Express*, June became very involved in the community. She joined the San Antonio Advertising Club and the Hill County Peace Officers Association. In 1951 she helped launch Theta Sigma Phi's Matrix Dinner, which recognized outstanding accomplishments in Southwest Texas. She also helped to organize a yearly clinic that provided publicity advice to civic, religious, and fraternal organizations. In 1952, she participated in a twenty-day junket with the Military Air Transport Service to military bases across Europe, with the purpose of encouraging women to consider a career in the armed services.

June and Jack's first date went well, and their relationship progressed quickly. They discovered a mutual admiration for each other's intelligence and creativity and found that their personalities were very similar, a mix of introspective depressiveness and smart-ass

Newlyweds Jack and June Kent in 1954. Courtesy of Jack Kent Jr.

irreverence. On 14 February 1954—after only half a year of knowing each other—the couple got engaged. For the wedding invitation, Jack drew a scene featuring his comic strip's two main characters: King Aroo: "June's a nice month for a wedding, Yupyop." Yupyop: "It's a nice name for a bride, too!"

They were married on June's thirty-fourth birthday at St. John's Lutheran Church, near La Villita Historic Arts Village. June's maid of honor was her friend and fellow *Express* reporter Anna Beth Morris. Jack's best man was fellow cartoonist and San Antonio radio personality Pat Boyette, who would go on to become a filmmaker and to draw comics for Charlton, Warren, and DC. After a reception at the Tapestry Room of the Saint Anthony Hotel, Jack and June headed to Mexico for their honeymoon.

Jack and Jackie Jr., 1955, Courtesy of Jack Kent Jr.

They ended up in Cuernavaca, a city just south of Mexico City, and nine hundred miles from San Antonio. In 1954 the population in Cuernavaca was about 40,000 people, much smaller than the over 300,000 people that live there now. Jack and June rented what June described in a note to *Express* columnist Bill Reddell as "a beautiful little house with a lovely garden and a small swimming pool." Their plan was to settle there permanently, but at the end of 1954 Kate Kilstofte had a heart attack. This, along with the fact that June had become pregnant, led the couple to pack up and head back north.

Jack, seemingly having learned his lesson from his brief marriage to Juliet, chose not to move back into the house on Johnson with Ralph and Peg. Instead, he and June found a place eight miles north in the new postwar suburbs at the corner of Gilbert Lane and Neer Avenue.

Jack began to anticipate his impending fatherhood in his work. A March 1955 storyline finds the flea family welcoming a new arrival. The baby flea disrupts life in the castle and prompts Yupyop to run away from home out of jealousy. As tends to happen in *King Aroo*, the storyline spins off in unexpected directions, in this case involving kidnapping and bloodhounds.

John Wellington Kent Jr. arrived on 20 July 1955. Jack heralded his son's arrival with a birth announcement to friends and family featuring Jackie Jr. in a bundle hanging from the mailbox and the punny caption "A little heir male for the Kents."

• • •

As Jack's personal life improved, *King Aroo*'s fortunes continued to dim, and relations between Jack and the syndicate became difficult and tense. In 1955, the *Times Colonist* in Victoria, British Columbia, dropped the strip after it scored low in a reader survey. Columnist Monte Roberts—who had praised Jack's work in 1953, saying, "Once King Aroo gets you, you're hooked for life"—wrote a column decrying the decision and calling on the paper's editor to "restore *King Aroo* to the throne." He went on, "*King Aroo* . . . is one of the funny things left on the funny pages. It is one of those rarities of rarities, a comic strip which is actually comic." The paper also printed a letter of support from a reader who wrote she would miss the "charming nonsense" of the strip. But in the following week's column, Roberts reported that his plea had not inspired an outcry of protest from readers and that *King Aroo* would not be returning to the paper.

Nearly a year later, an anonymous letter writer to the same paper complained about the removal of *King Aroo*, calling it "worthy of Lewis Carroll at his best." Also in Canada, *King Aroo* was still popular enough for students at Vancouver Technical School to include him in their newspaper-themed yearbook. And in the United States, a journalism student in Indiana named James H. Bowman used a *King Aroo* strip to write about New Year's resolutions. But readers such as this were clearly few and far between, and it was becoming clear that *King Aroo*'s reign was in danger of being cut short.

Chapter 7

My Future Looks Rosy, but Not Very Big! (1957–1960)

Though *King Aroo* was flagging commercially, Jack's devotion to the strip remained strong. Other than a brief period in the second half of 1955, when perhaps the sleep deprivation that comes with being a new parent caused Jack to be a little off his game, the strip maintained a high level of quality. Visually, things had changed dramatically over the years. All comic strips evolve over time as artists develop and refine their skills (or in some cases become complacent and/or pass work off to assistants), and characters settle into their final forms. In the case of *King Aroo*, the changes were not in character design but in Jack's cartooning style.

The dense, highly rendered Walt Kelly-inspired look was the norm for the strip's first year but gave way gradually to a looser approach closer to Jack's natural style. By 1953, the strip had a spacious appearance, with minimal shading, open backgrounds, and a judicious use of gray Ben Day dots, mostly to fill in Yupyop's suit. This simplification would continue into 1956 and 1957, as Jack abandoned his brush for a thin pen line.

Just as Jack simplified the strip visually over time, he also streamlined the presentation and content as well. By the time *King Aroo* went into its seventh year, daily strips were typically only two panels, with a setup in the first panel and the punch line in the second. The ongoing storylines of the early days gave way to one-off jokes or weeklong riffs on a certain theme. Whether this was a conscious effort to make the strip more accessible or a result of Jack's desire to put in fewer hours, it's not clear.

50 My Future Looks Rosy, but Not Very Big! (1957–1960)

One thing that didn't change was Jack's love of making allusions. Given that the residents of Myopia lived in an isolated fantasy land with one subscriber to the local newspaper and no public library (King Aroo accidentally made it disappear in the 30 Jan. 1955 strip), they were surprisingly well versed in songs, poetry, and literature. Of course this gives us a wonderful insight into what Jack was listening to and reading.

By virtue of *King Aroo*'s concept, allusions to fairy tales and fables proliferated. They ranged from the very well known ("Cinderella," "Jack and the Beanstalk," "Little Red Riding Hood") to the obscure (Joseph Jacobs's 1923 story "Fire! Fire! Burn Stick!"). Just as often, Jack used nursery rhymes, from "Old King Cole" to "Handy Dandy Jack-a-Spandy" to "Mary Mack." Adult literature and poetry also showed up fairly often, displaying the range of Jack's reading. There was the likes of Longfellow and Keats, *Rubaiyat of Omar Khayyam*, and *The Postman Always Rings Twice*.

Occasionally, there were mentions of songs, but these demonstrate that Myopia wasn't quick to embrace rock 'n' roll, or even swing, big band, or ragtime; Jack's tastes ran more toward classical music, operas, and musicals. By far, most of the songs alluded to in *King Aroo* were from the early 1900s, tunes like "In the Shade of the Old Apple Tree" and "A Bird in a Gilded Cage."

The remarkable thing wasn't so much that Jack brought these allusions into the comic pages but the way he wove them into his stories and jokes. Often he did it so cleverly that the success of the joke didn't even rely on the reader knowing that an allusion was being made. But the reader who *was* aware was rewarded with a deeper level of appreciation. Take for instance the 12 May 1953 strip. King Aroo is attending Queen Elizabeth II's coronation and asks Miss Pussy Cat what she did when she visited the queen. She responds, "I frightened a little mouse under her chair," and upon hearing this, King Aroo decides to bring the queen a mousetrap. This is a play on the English nursery rhyme "Pussy Cat, Pussy Cat" which goes:

> Pussy cat, pussy cat, where have you been?
> I've been to London to visit the queen.
> Pussy cat, pussy cat, what did you there?
> I frightened a little mouse under her chair.

Another example is from the strip's second storyline, in which Yupyop tries to evict pretend king Leo Lion from the castle. Yupyop writes, "Eeny meeny tekel upharsin" on the wall and says, "The handwriting's on the wall, Lion! Time to 'fess up!'" The strip moves on to Leo's admission that he's an impostor, but if one lingers on the words themselves for a moment one might find they're a play on "mene, mene, tekel, upharsin," the Aramaic writing that appears on the wall in the Bible story of Daniel in the lion's den (Daniel 5:25–31).

When it came to fairy tales, one of Jack's tricks was to introduce modern real-world concerns to the lives of the characters. In a 22 October 1952 strip, for instance, we learn that the fairy godmother went broke after Cinderella became a princess because "I was to get a 10% agent's commission, but like a fool I never got it down in writing." A 1951 strip tells us that the goose that laid the golden eggs had to start laying silver eggs (and then platinum eggs and then uranium eggs) when the United States went off the gold standard in 1933. Another 1951 strip brings media bias into the fable "The Tortoise and the Hare," with the hare claiming that he actually won the race and that the tortoise had cheated. "That sportswriter who covered the race (guy by the name of 'Aesop') got the facts mixed up in the story he wrote from the Athens Daily Bugle."

Sometimes Jack went to great lengths to set up his allusion as a groan-worthy pun, as in the 12 December 1953 strip, in which he depicted a sea eagle wearing a Greek chiton guarding a tollgate. King Aroo doesn't have any money to pay the toll, so he writes out an IOU: "Owed to a Grecian erne . . . 5¢." This being, of course, a play on the John Keats poem "Ode on a Grecian Urn." Similarly, there's the 11 November 1956 Sunday strip in which Wilbur the Mouse is portraying a gnome in a school play. While discussing the work it took to make his leaf-laden costume, he summarizes, "It takes a heap o' leaving to make a mouse a gnome." This was a reference to Edgar Albert Guest's 1916 poem "Home," and its first line, "It takes a heap o' livin' in a house t' make it home."

Allusions were a huge part of *King Aroo* and had the effect of reminding the reader they were reading a comic. Taking that even further was the fact that—like Krazy Kat and Ignatz before them—*King Aroo*'s characters occasionally showed an awareness that they resided in a comic strip. Though fictional characters making commentary on the medium they're in and breaking the fourth wall was known to happen in *Looney Tunes* shorts and Bob Hope/Bing Crosby *Road to . . .* movies, it was rarely seen on the comics page. The self-awareness of *King Aroo*'s characters allowed them to bend the rules of comic page physics. In the 29 April 1952 strip, a telephone appears right when it's needed, and Yupyop explains that it's "one of the conveniences of the medium we work in." Another strip finds Professor Yorgle staring at a big empty space and calling out, "Where's that joke we had, Yupyop?! We need it out here!"

Having his characters break the fourth wall also allowed Jack to make wry commentary about the medium. When someone falls over at the punch line in a 1960 strip, a doctor tells everyone that it's an atavistic impulse: "It's when we behave like our ancestors—time was when every comic strip ended with a 'plop!'" The 8 June 1954 episode finds King Aroo complaining that he hasn't appeared in his own strip for over a week. After a bit of a digression in a 1952 storyline, Yupyop says, "It's about time we got back to the plot, isn't it?"

Jack also liked to play with conventions visually. In a 1952 strip, Mr. Elephant tries to reverse his memory, and so his dialogue is written backward. In another instance, a character who's new to comic strips can't get the hang of placing his words inside the word balloons. And then there's poor Yupyop getting tangled in perspective lines during his visit to Hebefrenia.

• • •

March 1957 marked the end of Jack's *King Aroo* contract with McClure. The final storyline was a bit of metafiction that began with Mr. Elephant using a red balloon as a crystal ball. When King Aroo tries to blow it up, the balloon pops. "My future blew up in my face!" he exclaims. In subsequent strips, the king frets over having lost his future. It's impossible to not read it as Jack commenting on the apparent death of his dream. In the final *King Aroo* strip of the McClure run, Professor Yorgle opines, "Fate merely provides the tools—our future we build ourselves." As King Aroo begins to walk away, Yorgle says, "Where are you going?"

The king responds, "To get a building permit and start work."

It was a nice bit of closure for the devoted readers who were saying farewell, and a graceful and hopeful end. But it wasn't actually the end.

As his run with McClure was wrapping up, Jack got a call from George Stanleigh Arnold, an editor at the *San Francisco Chronicle*, which had run *King Aroo* since its inception and had given Jack a full-page profile in 1951. Stan, as he was known, was a huge *King Aroo* fan, finding its cleverness, visual wit, and kindheartedness exactly in line with his own sensibilities. He was even known, coincidentally, to wear a mustache virtually identical to that of King Aroo himself. He was also a generous champion of the underdog, so he offered Jack the chance to continue *King Aroo* in the *Chronicle*. Going from national syndication down to only one paper is a huge step backward, but it was Jack's only hope of keeping *King Aroo*—and his cartooning dreams—alive. As long as the strip survived, there was a chance, however small, that it could build momentum and go national again.

So from the second half of 1957 through late 1959, *King Aroo* would only appear in the *San Francisco Chronicle*. Jack didn't take the opportunity to radically reinvent the strip. *King Aroo* continued along the same trajectory as it had with McClure, with its plots and jokes continuing to become more streamlined.

Jack's drawing style also continued to become more and more economical. It's commonly accepted in cartooning that it takes more skill to use fewer lines, because you can't hide imperfections, so Jack's simplified style wasn't laziness as much as it was a growing confidence in his skills. After experimenting into early 1958 with the thin pen

King Aroo, 8 Mar. 1957. Courtesy of Jack Kent Jr.

line, Jack began using a brush again. With that change, Jack's style settled into its final form. There was more white space and the characters took on a cute, rounded look somewhat indebted to Charles Schulz and *Peanuts* but still unique and instantly recognizable. This simplified graphic style also happened to line up with what was going on in the comics page in general, with strips that had debuted in the mid- to late 1950s such as *Hi and Lois, Miss Peach,* and *B.C.*

• • •

While this was going on, the late 1950s were turning out to be a tough time for the Kent family. In August 1957 Kate Kilstofte passed away. She'd never fully recovered her health after her heart attack. June's brother Howard, who suffered PTSD from his experiences as an airplane mechanic in World War II, was disconsolate at the loss of his mother and began to drink heavily. At some point, he suffered a brain injury that would require him to be institutionalized at various Veterans Administration hospitals for the rest of his life. In the early days of his institutionalization, the family would drive to visit him in Galveston every weekend, nearly 250 miles each way. Howard would spend the rest of his life in VA hospitals around Texas, and Jack and June continued to visit him at least once a month.

Then, in early 1959, Ralph Kent died of congestive heart failure. He was just sixty-one years old. He'd been dismissed from his job at the Buckhorn when the Lone Star Brewing Company bought and moved the saloon to the grounds of their brewery, so in his final years, Ralph worked at a liquor store called Don's and Ben's. Jack idolized his father and was devastated by his death.

This was all on top of the family's bleak new financial reality. Jack had been paying three mortgages: one for the house on Gilbert, where he, June, and Jack Jr. lived; another on the house on Johnson Street; and the third for Happy and Kate's home (Happy had moved from working as a mason to a civil service job at Kelly Field Air Force base before retiring completely). Though Stan Arnold's dedication had single-handedly kept Jack's dream alive, the income from *King Aroo* was no longer enough to support the family's spending.

King Aroo, 30 Mar. 1956. Courtesy of Jack Kent Jr.

So Jack got a job at Ferguson Map Company in downtown San Antonio as a draftsman. Once Jack Jr. went off to school, June also got a job there, running the company's front desk and salesroom. Work on *King Aroo* was relegated to nights and weekends.

The family also made the decision to move into the house on Johnson Street. In her *Express* profile of Jack, June had written that the house seemed like "a completely comfortable place to live." Now she was going to test out the truth of her words. Since Peg Kent occupied the only bedroom, that left one big space to serve simultaneously as a dining room, living room, studio, and bedroom. For the latter, Jack and June folded out a sofa bed. When Jack Jr. was little his bed was "tucked behind a bookcase." Jack's piano also occupied the space. It was, as Jack Jr. would later say, "bohemian and intimate." After a couple of years of this situation, Jack and June added another room onto the house. This served, according to Jack Jr., as both his bedroom and a storage space.

Jack's "studio" consisted of a five-foot by six-foot secondhand wooden desk, with a lattice screen on which he hung his *Krazy Kat* original signed by George Herriman. His circle-bar-K brand was on display, as were dolls of King Aroo and Yupyop, created as prototypes for a toy line that never materialized. The desk itself was covered with various items Jack had collected and stored there, along with his pipe tray and a bottle of India ink. He'd prop a drawing board between his lap and the edge of the desk to do his actual work. If he needed a light table he'd use a sheet of glass with a shop light shining up from below.

• • •

A rare high point from this time period came courtesy of the Theta Sigma Phi Matrix Dinner that June had started and helped run each year. The keynote speaker at the 1959 edition was acclaimed cartoonist Edward D. Kuekes, who won the Pulitzer Prize in 1953 for a cartoon commenting on the Korean War (as two men carry a fallen soldier off the field one asks, "Wonder if he voted?" and the other responds, "No, he wasn't old enough"). Kuekes's main job was chief editorial cartoonist for the *Cleveland Plain Dealer*, but he also did strips, including *Do You Believe* (with Steve Freely, 1955–1962). In the 1930s he'd worked on a comic strip version of *Alice in Wonderland* as well as a short-lived Sunday comic called *Funny Fables*, which featured modern takes on fairy tales. With those credits, he and Jack surely found plenty of common ground, and indeed Jack introduced Kuekes at the dinner.

Chapter 8

Illogical Conclusions (1960–1965)

In early 1960 Stan Arnold took his devotion to *King Aroo* to the next level. His and Jack's plan to slowly rebuild interest in the strip had positive results, as other newspapers had begun to inquire about running *King Aroo*. Jack had turned them all down until the fall of 1959, when he allowed the *Lancaster Antelope Valley Ledger-Gazette* in California to run the strip. Seeing demand and opportunity, Arnold, along with his wife, Jane, formed their own syndicate, Golden Gate Features. Jack was their first and only client.

In April 1960 *King Aroo* began appearing nationally again in places like Tucson, Arizona; Madison, Wisconsin; and Hartford, Connecticut. With maps clearly on his mind, Jack created "King Aroo's Map of Clichés" as a promotional item for papers that took on the strip. It's hard to know exactly how Jack felt about this second chance at a national audience, but it's probably safe to say any optimism was tempered.

While still often absurd, whimsical, and pun filled, the tenor of *King Aroo* shifted in these later years. Jack seemed less and less interested in taking advantage of his fairy tale setting, with human characters appearing more often than animal ones. Jokes tended to be more obvious and pedestrian, such as a 10 May 1961 strip in which King Aroo takes a cucumber's temperature to see if it's cool. There's more mean-spiritedness and cynicism, which may have reflected Jack's own bitterness regarding the downturn in his cartooning fortunes, his father's death, and a general sense of pessimism.

King Aroo wasn't a strip, like *Pogo*, in which real-life events and concerns were part of the humor and storytelling. Timely items had

King Aroo, 2 Oct. 1961. An example of the strip becoming more mean-spirited. Courtesy of Jack Kent Jr.

King Aroo, 8 Jan. 1963. An example of Jack's cynicism at work. Courtesy of Jack Kent Jr.

occasionally popped up, but much more often Jack addressed real-world issues in general and nonspecific ways. And a lot of the time he did so with a cynical eye. Whether or not he would have defined himself as a cynic is hard to say, but Jack's comics of this time period frequently displayed a general distrust of people's motives, a pessimistic view of the world, and a curmudgeonly take on the way times were changing. This is especially true as the strip marched on into the early 1960s (and Jack into his forties), but it was there from very early on. In December 1950 strip, Leo Lion asks Yupyop what psychoanalysis is, and he replies, "A guessing game that's currently popular."

Throughout the strip's run, there are multiple indications that Jack thought humanity was on the wrong track. There are disparagements of radio advertising and television. Popular music was a target and so was the fact that postage was going up and that doctors had ceased to make house calls. The doubting Tomcat was often at the center

Illogical Conclusions (1960–1965)

of this (he claims to have been the first one to express doubts about "telephones and automobiles and radios, and instant puddings . . .").

Jack returned again and again to the idea that the world was in an awful state. A running gag was to have eggs refuse to hatch because they were swaddled in the newspaper or heard the news on the radio. In a 1963 strip a revived dodo bird decides to return to obscurity: "From what I've seen of the modern world, it's safer being extinct." In the 19 October 1960 strip, an argument about whether the Earth was round or flat resulted in King Aroo asking Professor Yorgle, "What is the shape of the world?" Yorgle answers, "Terrible," in a black speech bubble.

Jack's worries about the state of the world were likely due to the rising threat of nuclear war, the violence met by civil rights activists, and the Vietnam War. His experiences in World War II had turned him into a pacifist. When his nephew Kent revealed he was considering enlisting, Jack advised him specifically against joining the Army (Kent didn't listen; he'd become a captain and receive a bronze star for his service in Vietnam). Jack's aversion to violence showed up subtly in *King Aroo*, but it was definitely there. The occasional *Krazy Kat*-inspired beaning aside, Jack rarely showed characters in physical conflict. When Aroo battles Drexel Dragon to impress Beautiful Princess, the actual fight is covered by a card that reads "We spare the gentle reader the gruesome details of this bloody battle." If guns showed up in the strip, they were always pop guns. In an April 1964 entry, an angry man arrived to complain about the mismanagement of Myopia, blaming its obscurity on its peacefulness: "To attract any notice, a comic strip has to have violence and conflict!"

An 29 October 1964 strip may be his definitive statement on the issue. In it, King Aroo chats with Peace Dove.

> **Dove:** It's full time employment, reminding the more impetuous element that there's more to war than bugles and drums.
> **King Aroo:** Always somebody who needs reminding, eh?
> **Dove:** There's one born every minute.

Jack's cynicism and pessimism extended to politics, too. He harbored a general mistrust and disdain of elected officials, and this showed up sporadically in *King Aroo*. Two different times he used the line, "Politicians don't keep promises, promises keep politicians." In a 12 November 1962 strip, Professor Yorgle says, "Lincoln split rails to prepare for political office . . . nowadays the aspiring politician splits hairs."

Jack's most extended take on the topic is an April 1956 storyline in which Mr. Elephant decides to run against King Aroo to become ruler of Myopia (never mind that it's a monarchy, not a democracy). This sets up many jokes about political campaigns, including literal mudslinging and King Aroo going to work for Mr. Elephant's campaign in order to earn funds for his own. Probably the most cutting and still relevant of these is the 24 April strip in which the two candidates declare themselves to be on opposite sides of an issue before they've even learned what the issue is.

Jack's political views were not cut-and-dried. In an early 1980s *Contemporary Authors* questionnaire, he labeled himself as "conservative," but in an update just a couple of years later he shifted to "independent." According to Jack Jr., Jack was essentially a liberal Republican. In modern times this sounds like a complete oxymoron, but it was a sizable bloc of voters in the middle of the twentieth century, with this liberal offshoot of the Republican party personified by businessman and politician Nelson Rockefeller.

June's family had been members of the Minnesota Farmer–Labor Party, and as a result her political views were much more socialist and Democratic than her husband's. This often led to lively debate between the couple. In the 1968 presidential primaries, Jack and June

King Aroo, 17 Oct. 1960. The first of several times Mr. Elephant denies being a Republican. Courtesy of Jack Kent Jr.

made a deal that if the Republicans nominated Rockefeller over Richard Nixon, they'd both vote for him. Of course, Nixon ran away with the nomination.

Though socially more progressive than most Republicans, Jack was most passionately against the consolidation and misuse of power: big government, big labor, big corporations. The latter shows up in a 1952 *King Aroo* sequence where Professor Yorgle starts a business to challenge Wanda Witch's wish-granting monopoly. They end up in a price war that escalates to the point where Yorgle essentially replaces Wanda's monopoly with his own.

In his introduction to the *King Aroo* collection, Gilbert Seldes had written of Jack's "sly grace that gives an uncommon sweetness to all his work." It was true at the time Seldes wrote it, and it would be true again. But it wasn't true during the Golden Gate Features run of *King Aroo*. Jack's pessimism was not so much a personality trait or a terminal condition as it was likely a reaction to where his life was at the time. There was the ignominy of having to take on a map-making job after being a full-time cartoonist as well as the deaths of June's mother and Jack's father and the stress of weekly visits to Howard. On top of that, June's father, Happy Kilstofte, passed away in 1961. This would lead June to describe the late 1950s and early 1960s as "the time when everybody died."

And history was repeating itself with *King Aroo*. Just as before, the strip was failing to catch on to a wide audience. Though his cartooning was as strong or stronger than ever, Jack seemed to become somewhat disengaged from his own creation. He even began to recycle jokes. There's a thin line between running gags and simply repeating jokes, and Jack did both.

Nearly every comic strip has running gags: jokes and scenarios that repeat periodically. Think of Lucy pulling the football away from Charlie Brown, Garfield's dislike of Mondays, Dagwood taking a nap on his couch, or the Not Me ghost in *Family Circus*. These offer a comfortable predictability to readers and serve as a shortcut for the cartoonist, who is charged with generating a never-ending stream of new stories and jokes. One might say that the more numerous and memorable the running gags a strip has, the more likely it is to become a hit.

King Aroo—perhaps to its own detriment commercially—didn't do running gags in any sort of traditional way, but there were jokes and premises that Jack returned to again and again, including Mr. Elephant's poor memory, Yupyop sending King Aroo to sit in the corner for bad behavior, caterpillars and polliwogs, flea circuses, crossword puzzles, Wanda Witch's soup being mistaken for potions, shadows operating independently of their owners, cuckoo clocks, and cats having nine lives. Jack also liked to revisit certain idioms, such as "a bird in the hand is worth two in the bush," "building castles in the sky," and "one swallow doesn't make a summer."

It does appear that early on Jack attempted to start a catchphrase of sorts. While playing at moose hunting in the strip's first storyline, Yupyop declares: "Tally Ho! Yoicks! And similar quaint hunting expressions." Nine months later the Carpenter Bird gets on his newly built house boat and says, "Avast! Belay! Shiver me timbers! And similar salty sayings!" The makings of a running gag were there, but Jack didn't return to it for another seven months, and it then showed up four months in a row in different variations. The last appearance was in 1953, when a baby flea says, "Goo! And similar infantile expressions."

But post-1960 there were also jokes that just plain repeated themselves. It was a strange state of affairs for a cartoonist whose syndicate once bragged that he had "more ideas every day than he can use in a month of drawing" and whose early *King Aroo* comics often had multiple jokes layered within a single strip. Jack was surely aware that he'd used these jokes before, so why repeat? Well, the fact that he was holding down a full-time job while also producing a daily comic gave him less time to devote to generating new material. He also likely figured it was a very small number of readers who would have read the strip since its inception and even a smaller number who would have a long enough memory to recognize the recycled punch lines.

In most cases Jack repeated the setups and jokes wholesale, with only the drawings differing. But in other cases, Jack refined and improved the joke the second time through. For instance, one panel in the 11 November 1951 Sunday strip finds King Aroo stating, "I can play 'Marching through Georgia' . . . except I have a bit of trouble with the part between Macon and Savannah." Professor Yorgle advises,

"Next time try Route 80—it's paved all the way." When Jack revisited the joke nearly ten years later on 11 July 1961, Professor Yorgle was replaced by a pair of birds. The lines are delivered exactly the same, but this time the second bird adds, "When they finish Interstate 16 it'll be a breeze."

Jack even acknowledged the fact that he was reusing jokes. In a 1961 strip Yupyop comes across King Aroo burning a pile of old jokes and tells him to stop because they may need them. Likewise in a 24 September 1963 strip a mind reader tells King Aroo that his thoughts are the same as they were at his last reading a year before. King Aroo replies, "I know—fact is, I haven't had a new thought in years!"

In addition to revealing Jack's cynicism and lack of engagement, *King Aroo* was starting to betray Jack's bitter mindset about his cartooning fortunes. A 1963 entry posited that publicity, advertising, promotion, and propaganda were "a very satisfactory substitute for quality and talent." And an early 1965 storyline finds all of the characters feeling like nobodies. The 8 February edition seemed to have special resonance for Jack's situation. Professor Yorgle tells Yupyop, "I know what it's like to be a nobody—all my life I was a nobody—but I didn't really care. But then I got ambition!"

"And now you're somebody?" Yupyop asks.

"No!" Yorgle replies, "Now I'm miserable being nobody!"

Given all of that, it's no surprise what happened next. Though it's likely that Stan Arnold would have supported *King Aroo* as long as Jack wanted to keep making it (much in the way William Randolph Hearst had subsidized George Herriman and *Krazy Kat*), Jack wasn't happy with the way things were headed. "One day," he said, "I simply looked at the calendar and saw how old I was getting." Forty-four wasn't old, of course, but he likely looked ahead and couldn't fathom twenty plus more years of working full time and creating a comic strip for a few devoted fans. So he made the momentous decision to end *King Aroo*.

The final installment appeared on 14 June 1965 signed, "With all my love, Jack Kent." Jack Jr., then just shy of his tenth birthday, witnessed his dad inking the farewell strip on the verge of tears.

And then, right on the heels of one life-changing decision, Jack made another one. He quit his job at Ferguson. For the third, and final, time in his life, he threw his career fortunes to the fates.

Part 2

Chapter 9

From *Humpty Dumpty* to *Playboy* (1965–1968)

If Jack had written out his philosophy of life, two tenets would certainly have been (1) Don't put limitations on what you can accomplish if you are willing to work for it ("Work is a form of magic—you can accomplish miracles with it," a bird wisely informs us in the 18 Jul. 1955 *King Aroo*); and (2) There is so much to learn about the fascinating world we live in. Both of these played out explicitly in the months and years after Jack ended *King Aroo*.

One way Jack sought knowledge about the world was through books. Just as he had as a young man, Jack continued to haunt his favorite bookstores and read ravenously about a wide range of topics. He expected the same of Jack Jr., who recalled, "Whatever I asked about when I was little, he tried to answer, and then referred me to the encyclopedias and dictionaries he'd picked up in used book stores. No excuses: The answer is out there."

Travel was another way Jack tried to learn about the world's places and people. So his first instinct upon quitting both of his jobs in 1965 was not to start job seeking but to pack up the family for a sojourn to Europe. As the story goes, Jack and June had gone out to lunch together and were walking up the stairs back to Ferguson Maps when both of their knees popped simultaneously. This prompted a joint realization that time was getting away from them and that they needed to see some more of the world while they were still able to.

So Jack and June both quit their jobs and remortgaged the house at 103 Johnson. By that point they'd paid off their initial mortgage, so this gave them some cash to work with. They ordered a Volkswagen Beetle to be picked up at the factory in Wolfsburg, Germany, and requested permission from the principal at Jack Jr.'s school for him to miss the first couple of months of fifth grade. They set off in the fall of 1965, beginning their journey in New York, where they attended the second year of the World's Fair and went sightseeing. From there they flew to Amsterdam and took a train to Germany to pick up the Beetle.

They bought a copy of Frommer's *Europe on $5 a Day*, not only to save money but to avoid doing the typical American tourist thing. After Germany they went to Kolding, Denmark and visited some of June's family. Then it was on to Austria, Switzerland, Italy, France, back to Amsterdam, and then across to England. Jack, with his love of languages, tried his hand at Danish, Italian, French, and German as they traveled.

• • •

When the Kents arrived back home in late fall 1965, Jack faced the reality of the big gamble he'd taken. As he had twice before—after dropping out of high school and when returning home after World War II—Jack set about building a career from the ground up. And just as he had back then, he approached being a freelancer by saying yes to everything. "I've always said that if you are a free-lance and you're caught up, that's tantamount to being unemployed," he'd comment later. That's how he ended up producing patent drawings for a new type of airline toilet on behalf of a local inventor (the patent was denied), driving a delivery truck, and creating greeting cards for Hallmark.

Meanwhile, June returned to work at the *San Antonio Express*, serving mainly as a copyeditor for the news desk and as editor of supplements to the Sunday magazine. Though their work life was now very different, other aspects of the Kents' life continued as usual. One- or two-week trips to Mexico were a regular summer occurrence. On one of these trips, they had a chance encounter with cartoonist Gus Arriola—creator of the strip *Gordo*—in a motel swimming pool in Tehuantepec. Gus was also on vacation with his family. The cartoonists recognized one another immediately and struck up a conversation and a subsequent friendship through the mail.

In the summer of 1967 the Kents took a two-week vacation north to attend Montreal Expo '67. They drove and didn't make reservations ahead of time. June wrote about the Expo for the *Express*: "It's a tremendous show, done with wit, intelligence, imagination, taste. It's a sample of what our world has to offer, and if your horizons aren't widened, it's because your mind is closed." Attending the Expo was also what convinced twelve-year-old Jack Jr., who up to that point had wanted to be scientist, to follow his mother's ambition to study architecture.

Though he was finding paying work where he could get it, Jack's overall focus was still on comic strips. He held out hope that he could create a new daily feature that a syndicate would be interested in. He generated a handful of proposals during this time. One was *Skittles*, a *Peanuts*-like strip following the adventures of a boy, a girl, and their dog. This, and indeed all of Jack's proposals, went unsold.

But starting in 1967, he did begin to have success landing one-panel comic strips in magazines, including *Parade* and *Playboy*. Jack's comic in the July 1967 issue of *Playboy* features a small boy sailing his toy boat in a pond. On a nearby rock sits a nude five-year-old girl strumming a harp like a siren.

Jack was a regular reader of *Playboy*. "I read it for the articles" went the common refrain, but in Jack's case it was "I read it for the cartoons." The magazine was known for paying cartoonists well, and only a portion of its cartoons were salacious. In fact, *Playboy* sported work by many a children's illustrator: Shel Silverstein, Syd Hoff, Don Madden, Tomi Ungerer, Jules Fieffer, Bernard Wiseman, Lee Lorenz, B. Tobey, Charles E. Martin, Rowland B. Wilson, and George Booth. Outside of Madden and Silverstein, these cartoonists' work in *Playboy* rarely contained nudity or sex.

A couple of months later, Jack landed a piece in a very different sort of publication, *Humpty Dumpty's Magazine for Little Children*. A bit of verse called "Puppies," about a home overrun by canines, represents Jack Kent's first work created expressly for children. The poem is funny, but its most surprising and charming quality is the illustrations, which were not provided by Jack but by twelve-year-old Jack

A page from "Puppies," a father-son collaboration that saw print in *Humpty Dumpty's Magazine,* October 1967. Courtesy of Jack Kent Jr.

Jr. The idea for the piece arose when Jack Jr. had a dream about puppies and the next day drew what he'd seen in his dream. Jack wrote a poem to go with the drawings, Jack Jr. added a few more drawings to go with the poem, and then Jack inked over his son's pencil work.

The piece came from experience. The Kents had two dogs. Gus was a small, mostly white mutt, who Jack Jr. thinks may have just shown up at the house one day as a young stray. Toggle was a female dachshund given to Jack Jr. on his seventh birthday. Once Toggle arrived she "quickly became queen of us all," Jack Jr. says. That included Gus, whom she regularly outsmarted for food, bones, and attention. She lived until 1980.

A pair of Jacks at the house on Johnson Street, 1969. Courtesy of Jack Kent Jr.

Jack Jr.'s drawings for "Puppies," done with an ink line and a flat single color applied mostly in the background, show he'd inherited more than a little of his father's visual wit. For example, a dog in the den cocks its ear at an old style gramophone, and in the bedroom, a poodle admires itself in the mirror. As cute as the collaboration between father and son was, the publication of "Puppies" wasn't without a tiny bit of controversy. Jack Jr. says of his father, "He was both amused and a little hurt that they paid me a lot more than him since he'd given me sole credit for the illustrations—illustrators got more than writers. I hope they used whatever I got for groceries—goodness knows we needed money at that point."

Later, Jack would describe Jack Jr. as "the artist in the family" and "the best cartoonist in the country."

• • •

Jack's breakthrough year, in several ways, was 1968. In addition to another *Playboy* cartoon in the March issue (this one depicting a young woman in a Mayan sacrificial ceremony, with one female bystander commenting to another, "Takes some of the incentive out of being a virgin, doesn't it?") he landed comics in several different issues of the *Saturday Evening Post* between April and December. These ranged from lowbrow (a caption-free picture of a chubby girl painting a svelte bikini body onto her oversized shirt) to highbrow (a piece titled "Author! Author!" depicting different kinds of writers, such as a butler writing a "whodunit" mystery). Jack also briefly joined the "gang of usual idiots" at *Mad Magazine*. His first piece—appearing in the July 1968 issue—was a six-panel wordless comic called "A Modern Cinderella," an updated take on the classic fairy tale that was right out of the *King Aroo* playbook. In it, the fairy godmother grants Cinderella's wish, but a ball gown isn't to her liking. On the second try the godmother gives her a red minidress, green striped tights, flat shoes with a ball on top, and a late sixties-style pixie haircut. *Mad* chose to assign a different artist—mainstay Jack Rickard—to carry out Jack's vision.

A few months later, it would be both his words and his pictures in a two-page feature called "A Mad Look at Sex Education in the Schools." The piece was a collection of seven black-white-and-gray wash pantomime gags on the topic, such as a boy having to sit in the corner wearing a dunce cap because he drew a picture of the stork bringing a baby. One finds a young lad doing his homework assignment by peeking at his sister in the shower, and another getting his mouth washed out with soap for repeating what he learned at school. The *King Aroo* "Teechur" character makes an appearance in the feature's header, though given a significant breast augmentation. The inherent cuteness of Jack's cartooning style was a perfect match with the subject matter, preventing the affair from descending into exploitation.

From *Humpty Dumpty* to *Playboy* (1965–1968)　　　73

Jack would place four more pieces in *Mad Magazine*, stretching into early 1970, three with *Mad* legend Paul Coker Jr. and another with Jack Rickard. Jack even flew to New York to visit the *Mad* offices, and there he met a fan. Cartoonist Sergio Aragonés, who was born in Spain and grew up in Mexico City, had worked for *Mad* since 1963, and was best known for his wordless cartoons in the margins of the magazine's features. Aragonés had long admired *King Aroo*, having discovered the strip in high school. He couldn't read English then but was taken with the visuals, "I had never seen such a tender and simpatico way to draw people and animals, the simplicity of the backgrounds." Jack and Sergio had lunch in New York, and the admiring younger cartoonist inundated Jack with questions, a heartening reversal of Jack's earlier fawning over George Herriman.

Jack's other pieces in *Mad* were similar to the ones that came before. The three with Coker were collections of cartoons on a topic: "A Mad Look at Frustration" (including a princess kissing a frog who then transforms into an old king), "You Know You're Really Overweight When . . ." (". . . you give up your seat to an old lady . . . and two old ladies sit down"), and "You Know You're Really Nobody When . . ." (". . . you grow a mustache and nobody even notices it"). The one he did with Rickard was another one-pager, featuring a knight in armor falling down the stairs, jarring him so much that his feet end up poking out of the head hole.

Jack would later claim that around the same time he placed work in *Playboy*, *Humpty Dumpty's Magazine*, and others, he had also landed a one-panel gag in the *New Yorker*. This would have been a huge deal, as the magazine was basically the top of the mountain for cartoonists. But a thorough search of the *New Yorker*'s cartoon archive shows no evidence of a Jack Kent comic. The most likely explanation, then, is the same as it was for his elusive teenage *Collier's* cartoon: either Jack sold a cartoon that never saw print, or his idea was adapted by one of the magazine's established cartoonists.

The year 1968 also found Jack returning to the daily comics, if only for one month. One of the ideas Jack tried to sell to syndicates was a space-age comic strip called *A-OK*. It concerned an astronaut named Topo who becomes stranded on a flat planet called Tweenkle. Among the planet's residents are King Ling—whose crown is a teapot—and his adviser Erskill, who does all of the king's thinking for him. It was essentially *King Aroo* in space.

As topical as that was with NASA's Apollo program in full swing (something that Jack took great personal interest in), *A-OK* wasn't picked up by a syndicate. Instead, the Newspaper Enterprise Association hired Jack to use the characters in a twenty-strip Christmas-themed storyline they'd offer to papers across the country that December. "Why Christmas Almost Wasn't" was, in many ways, a return to the heyday of *King Aroo*. There were puns, mythical characters who are faced with reality (Santa says he's had to expand his delivery area "since folks started gadding about in space" and might need to go self-service), ridiculous situations (the Christmas tree keeps running away), surprising transformations (Santa becomes a rag doll), and characters that are aware they're in a comic strip (Topo is so surprised when he sees Santa Claus he falls off panel and almost off the edge of the planet).

The story concerned Santa coming to visit Tweenkle and finding all the Christmas spirit has been drained away by the animosity between King Ling and the Woofers, who live on the underside of the planet. The ultimate solution finds the two sides putting aside their differences and sharing Christmas together. But it's not all warm and fuzzy. King Ling announces, "But after Christmas we'll dislike each other again, of course" and the King Woofer agrees. It's a turn away from the sometimes-cynical tone of the later years of *King Aroo*, but not a drastic one. Topo delivers the moral: "That's how it goes, I'm afraid. We put love on the menu at Christmas, but too often there aren't many leftovers."

Why Christmas Almost Wasn't, 6 Dec. 1968. Courtesy of Jack Kent Jr.

"Why Christmas Almost Wasn't" was a stealth pilot for an ongoing strip; had response been thunderous it may very well have fulfilled Jack's second shot at achieving his cartooning dreams. But things didn't work out that way, and "Why Christmas Almost Wasn't" instead served as Jack's last appearance on the comics page. By the time the feature ran in newspapers, Jack had already embarked on a new career that would consume the rest of his life.

Chapter 10

The Sandbox Set (1968–1970)

Jack was one of those semirare people who grow up without losing their fascination with children's books. Though he was a great admirer and student of children's illustrations and storytelling, Jack rarely talked about the books that spoke to him as a child. One could assume that he was exposed to a wide variety of Mother Goose nursery rhymes and fairy and folktales by the likes of Hans Christian Andersen, Aesop, and Brothers Grimm. He was a fan of A. A. Milne; *Winnie-the-Pooh* came out when Jack was six years old, so it's very likely he read it and its 1928 sequel *The House at Pooh Corner*, when he was a boy.

As evidenced by his nephew Kent's discoveries in Jack's bedroom at the Maurer, Jack kept up with new picture books as an adult and was continually adding to his collection. It seems he may have been slightly embarrassed about this, but with Jack Jr.'s arrival, he said, "I had the justification and that made it all look rational." If the lover of children's books is like a person with a sweet tooth, having a child is like moving into a candy factory. As Jack would write later, "Those of us who have been snitching our kids' books to admire them for their graphics will agree . . . that this is a genuine art form."

Jack Jr. says his father had three sections of the family library devoted to artists he admired, one of fine art (Miro, Picasso, Dalí, Klee, etc.), one of cartoons (which was heavy on *New Yorker* cartoonists), and one of children's books, with work by Arthur Rackham, Alice and Martin Provensen, and Ronald Searle, among others. Jack also admired or would come to admire the works of author-illustrators

Quentin Blake, Joseph Low, Margot Zemach, Lisl Weil, Tomi Ungerer, and Miroslav Sasek and writers Joan Aiken and Lewis Carroll. "You'll see a similarity in those in that they all deal in light whimsy," he said.

Some of Jack's favorite contemporary cartoonists had also made children's books. Walt Kelly illustrated John O'Reilly's *The Glob* in 1952. *Barnaby*'s Crockett Johnson had illustrated books by Margaret Wise Brown and his wife, Ruth Krauss (the aforementioned *The Carrot Seed*), in the 1940s but had started a children's book career in earnest with 1955's *Harold and the Purple Crayon*. The *New Yorker* cartoonist William Steig put out his first children's books in 1968.

But the clearest antecedent to Jack's transition from cartoonist to children's author was Johnny Gruelle (1880–1938). Gruelle started out as a staff cartoonist for newspapers in his hometown of Indianapolis and then landed a syndicated strip, *Mr. Twee Deedle* (1911–1914). While also doing work for magazines (including intricate bird's-eye pieces set in the fictional Yapp's Crossing and Yahoo Center), he began to create illustrations for fairy tale collections. *Raggedy Ann Stories*, based on an actual doll Gruelle himself created, was published in 1918 and spawned a host of fantastical sequels. Gruelle's work was humorous, whimsical, and full of wordplay. His illustrations were described by his biographer, Patricia Hall, as "bright and fluid . . . crisply captured with pen and brush."

The broad strokes of Gruelle's professional life could just as easily have described Jack's, and Jack counted *Raggedy Ann Stories* as a beloved childhood favorite. In a 1941 article in the *San Antonio Light*, Gruelle was among the cartoonists about whom Jack shared bits of trivia he'd gathered. And in a 1969 review of Constantine Georgiou's *Children and Their Literature*, Jack lamented the book's omission of Gruelle's work.

Jack started working on his first children's book, *Just Only John*, not long after the family returned from their two-month Europe trip in late summer 1965. But even with his professional credentials, it would be a long road to becoming published.

The idea for *Just Only John* had come to Jack in the late 1950s, when Jack Jr. was four and a half years old. With a full-time job and *King Aroo* to focus on, Jack set his idea aside. He picked it back up in late 1965 and fleshed it out into a full-blown dummy. For the painted

An early study for *Just Only John*, ca. 1966. Jack Kent Papers. Kerlan Collection, Children's Literature Research Collections, University of Minnesota Libraries, Minneapolis. Courtesy of Jack Kent Jr. and the Kerlan Collection.

pictures, he tried to emulate the approach he most commonly saw in popular picture books of the day: bold graphic illustrations inspired by modern art.

Jack sent out his manuscript to publisher after publisher and was met with rejection after rejection. After over twenty no-thank-yous, he finally got a whiff of interest. In submitting pieces to *Humpty Dumpty*, Jack had established a relationship with editor Alvin Tresselt. *Humpty Dumpty* was owned and operated by *Parents' Magazine*, which since the 1940s had also operated Parents' Magazine Press, publishing comic books and children's books. Tresselt liked *Just Only John*'s story (indeed the published version is nearly a word-for-word match to Jack's original draft) but not its illustrations. Tresselt—an

From an early draft of *Just Only John*, ca. 1966. Jack Kent Papers. Kerlan Collection, Children's Literature Research Collections, University of Minnesota Libraries, Minneapolis. Courtesy of Jack Kent Jr. and the Kerlan Collection.

accomplished children's author with a Caldecott Medal on his resume (1947's *White Snow, Bright Snow* with Roger Duvoisin)—had become executive editor and vice-president of Parents' Magazine Press in 1965.

Over the course of a year, Jack reworked *Just Only John* under Tresselt's guidance. And as he did it, he found that he hadn't needed to change his cartooning style to make children's books. In the winter of 1966 he sent a note explaining that in the course of doing several quick sketches of a little boy for another project, he'd hit on what Tresselt was looking for. "By then I had worked it back to my natural style. It was like my comic strip art, and that's what they wanted all along." Parents' Magazine Press finally offered him a contract.

The story finds young John bored with being himself. So he goes to the shop of Mrs. Walpurgis, who does "witchcraft and hemstitching," and buys a mystery magic spell for a penny. This ends up turning him into whatever others might suggest. So when his mother calls him "little lamb," well you can guess what happens. After various transformations and a visit to Daddy, young John realizes he's happiest being himself. Jack adds the Aesop-like moral, "Be yourself, because somebody has to, and you're the closest."

The book has several clever little turns of phrase such as this, as well as cute visual gags. For instance, the narrator tells us, "Daddy was a very important man, with his own office and his name on the door" and sure enough there on the office door is stenciled "Daddy." Jack used a thick brush line and heavy watercolors that, even after a year of reworking, wasn't quite his natural style but was still very pleasing.

Just Only John—dedicated to its inspiration, Jack Jr.—appeared in bookstores in July 1968. Reviews were good and the book sold well, eventually moving nearly half a million copies. Outside of the brief, heady, early days of *King Aroo*, Jack had labored largely underappreciated as a cartoonist. Now, as a children's author, he had discovered instant widespread acceptance. "I was flabbergasted," he said of the response. Besides the sales, the book won two awards, one from the Chicago Graphics Associates and one from the Children's Book Clinic.

By Jack's great luck, 1968 was a perfect time to start writing children's books. Title II of the Elementary and Secondary Education Act, passed into law in 1965, provided schools and libraries with significant funds for buying children's books. As a result, publishers saw their sales skyrocket, and the demand for new titles rose dramatically. It seems getting interest in *Just Only John* inspired Jack to work up other ideas for children's books and then send them winging across the country to publishers before waiting for his first book to hit stores. Within six months of the release of *Just Only John*, Jack had published not only his second children's book but his third and fourth as well. *Fly Away Home*, *Mr. Elephant's Birthday Party*, and *Clotilda* all came out in early spring 1969, each published by a different publisher. This was an impressive feat for an author working without an agent.

Fly Away Home, published by David McKay, was based on the English nursery rhyme "Ladybird Ladybird," specifically the "ladybug" variation that Jack had used in *King Aroo* on two separate occasions. The simple tale involves a girl trying to help a ladybug, whom she has dubbed "Mrs. Mildred," find a home and learning about habitats along the way. In a sharp contrast from his illustrative work on *Just Only John*, here Jack uses a scratchy pen line and only one color (a deep red) for accents. His tendency to add clever bits for adult appreciation

The Sandbox Set (1968–1970)   81

continues, though, such as when the girl gets frustrated at Mrs. Mildred's lack of a vocal response: "A conversation isn't a conversation if only one person is doing it," she scolds. "It's more like a *recitation*."

Jack sweetly dedicated the book to June and Jack Jr., "who make *my* house 'home.'"

All of Jack's first four children's books had themes or ideas that had previously appeared in *King Aroo*, but none more so than *Mr. Elephant's Birthday Party*, published by Houghton Mifflin. It's one of only two of Jack's children's books to use both a storyline *and* characters from the strip. In addition to Mr. Elephant, there's Mr. Pennipost the kangaroo, Doubting Thomas the cat, and Harold Rooster. The story mirrors a *King Aroo* plot from September 1951 in which Mr. Elephant finds a birthday card and, being so forgetful by nature, believes that it's his birthday. This leads to a party, where his friends each present him with a unique gift. Harold the Rooster gives Mr. Elephant the remains of the shell he hatched from (it was an Easter egg). Doubting Thomas gives him a page from a book of nursery rhymes about the cow jumping over the moon ("It was the first thing I ever doubted," he reveals), and Mr. Pennipost gives him postcards of Australia. Since Mr. Elephant has no memories of his own, each friend has given him a memento from their own lives. It's very touching. Jack dedicated the book to his mother.

As with its source material, the book is full of little and big jokes, such as when Mr. Elephant, having forgotten it's his own party he's going to, wraps up his hat for a present. When he opens it he says, "It's a hat! Just what I needed! I gave *away* the one I *had*." It was Jack's third book and his third different art style. He returned to the thick brush of *Just Only Jack* but rendered his characters and objects with only partial outlines, letting the flat colors (only gold and reddish brown) do everything else. It gives the book a striking graphic look.

An October 1952 *King Aroo* featured an out of work fairy godmother, and Jack returned to that idea for *Clotilda*, published by Random House as a small (6" × 6") black-and-white hardcover. When Tommy and Betty come across Clotilda, she's sitting on a daisy "feel[ing] sorry for herself in comfort." Tommy is immediately dismissive, calling her a bug because he doesn't believe in fairy godmothers. He's not even convinced by her acts of magic (which admittedly are based in reality, such as a polliwog becoming a frog), so she turns him into a donkey. Betty's kindness, on the other hand, earns her three wishes. She uses one to gain a promise that she'll grow up to be just like her mother, another to change Tommy back to a boy, and the last one to request that Clotilda be her personal fairy godmother forever.

It's a deceptively simple story about the power of open-mindedness ("The world is full of magic and anyone who can't appreciate it is a donkey!") and the benefits of kindness. This was a sharp turnaround from the cynical later days of *King Aroo*, reflecting the renewed sense of optimism Jack was feeling in both his life and his work.

Things were looking up for the Kents in 1969. Besides Jack's new career as an author, June was promoted to editor of the Sunday magazine and the features sections of the *Express*. The family settled into a routine. Jack typically awoke around 5:30 in the morning and took his time getting started. He'd have a pipe and his coffee while reading the newspaper. He'd drive Jack Jr. and June to school and work, run any necessary errands, and then settle into his armchair to sketch out ideas in pencil on old blueprint paper from his days at Ferguson. He'd eat lunch with his mother, usually on the back terrace as long as the weather cooperated.

After picking up Jack Jr. and June, he'd indulge in a cigar—which he smoked down to a nub that then went into the pipe, wasting nothing—and the evening newspaper. After dinner he'd read or watch TV. His actual work on his books didn't start until the rest of the family was settled in bed. While June slept three feet away in the hideaway, he'd burn the midnight oil. To the rest of the family's chagrin, he refused to have air conditioning in the house, working without a shirt and fighting off green gnats that flew to his floodlight. So part of the answer to how a person makes so many books in such a short time is that they sacrifice sleep.

Jack also had to quickly develop an efficient creative process.

His story ideas usually started on index cards, which Jack would then file in used cigar boxes (given his habit, there was a constant supply, and he didn't like to waste a good box). As much as possible he would try to write and visualize the story simultaneously. Next he would produce what he called a "manuscribble"—a manuscript with drawings—ensuring that the text and art were inseparable. He'd type out the text painstakingly with two fingers on a manual typewriter, cut out the text, and rubber cement it on Strathmore boards.

He'd then sketch out the illustrations in either pencil or pen. It wasn't always easy. "If I could just put on paper what I see in my mind, that would be great," he said. "But it doesn't work out that way."

Jack would send a manuscribble to editors once they'd expressed interest in an idea. When it came time to produce final illustrations, he would often just tweak the manuscribble. He sketched first in non-photo blue pencil, then finalized the ink line with either a camel's hair brush or a crow quill pen. In the early days before preseparation of color, he'd have to create the illustrations using not the actual colors themselves but percentages of gray that represented cyan, yellow, and magenta, each on its own mylar overlay taped to a piece of glass that served as a table. The more colors Jack wanted in a book, the more of a guessing game it became, as colors didn't always turn out how he intended. He could also control the level of transparency by how thick or thin he applied the paint. As technology progressed in the 1970s, he was able to work on some books in watercolor or transparent inks on a single sheet.

Jack labored over the text in his books—"I'll write a line in which I have maybe five or six alternate words in one spot in a sentence," he said, "to decide later which of those words ought to be used"—and thus didn't always respond well to editors' suggestions about wording. But since the feedback came in writing, Jack was able to move past his initial reaction and take time to think about what was being asked of him and how he might be able to defend his choice, go along with the editor, or compromise.

• • •

The Grown-Up Day was Jack's fourth book of 1969, his fifth children's book overall, and his second for Parents' Magazine Press. It was Jack's first book to be written in verse instead of prose. The story is based on the premise of children pretending to be grown-ups, which Jack used to create a sly send-up of adult behavior. The lead characters, brother and sister, don't just wear their parents' clothes and play house but say and do the same things, such as making the dog, doll, and teddy

84   The Sandbox Set (1968–1970)

bear children wash their hands and faces before eating or telling them, "run along and play. I've got lots of work to do." The brother reads the paper and says things like, "Dear, dear!" and "Goodness me! What are we coming to?" The children in the book clearly relish being able to switch between being kids and being grown-ups. It's a benefit we mostly lose as we become adults, but Jack realized that in his new career he had the opportunity to revisit being a kid.

The illustrations were Jack's simplest so far, with a thin loose pen line, pale watercolors, and no backgrounds at all. His marriage of text and pictures is strong, such as when the brother implores the teddy bear to take his medicine and tries it himself to prove it doesn't taste bad. "It's really rather good," he says, as a parent would, but his face is scrunched up in disgust.

In addition to his books and his *Mad Magazine* pieces, Jack also placed at least three cartoons in national newspapers in 1969. In the sweet "The Last Analysis," a therapist listens to and reassures his patient and then heads home, where his wife listens to and reassures him. In "Cut to the Quick," a man pays extra for long-stemmed roses, only to have his sweetheart trim the stems to put them in a vase. And "Inflation" finds a woman taking out a loan in order to afford her groceries.

Jack continued his frantic publishing pace into 1970, with three more books, two of which explored different aspects of imagination. *The Blah*, published by Parents' Magazine Press, is about using fantasy to work through difficult emotions. Billy feels ignored and forgotten by his family, especially his brother Richard, who jostles him and steps on his green crayon. Billy labels himself a "Blah" and begins to draw a legion of other Blahs, potato-shaped creatures with stick arms and legs. Then he puts himself and his fellow Blahs into an adventure where they first help others who've been victims of the "Terrible, Awful Jostler" and then move on to a showdown with the big baddie himself. Billy the Blah sends the Jostler tumbling into a lake, and the other Blahs smash his crayons. The color on this sequence is done with a crayon texture, cleverly demarcating it as make-believe.

Billy's revenge fantasy is cathartic but would be somewhat disturbing if not for the ending of the book. Billy's mother brings him out of his reverie by telling him to get ready for supper. The fact that she had to say this multiple times before he listened has frustrated her: "Sometimes you act as if you don't even know I'm around," she says. Billy smiles, kisses her, and tells her she can be Queen of the Blahs. This ending is ambiguous and can be interpreted multiple ways, but it seems to indicate that the act of imagining and creating has broken Billy out of his funk, and now he's advising his mother to do the same.

In tribute to its themes of sibling rivalry, Jack dedicated *The Blah* to his sister, Mary Lou. The two had remained close into adulthood and shared a sense of whimsy and a strong creative drive. Mary Lou painted, sewed, and wrote. Settled with her family (which had grown two children larger with daughter Judy and son Carter joining Kent) in Shreveport, Louisiana, Mary Lou began writing articles for the *Shreveport Journal* and served as president of the local writers' club. She won club awards for her poetry and short stories (one with the colorful and intriguing title "The Supererogatory Electronic Love Charm"). Later in her life, she started puppeteering, eventually joining the Puppeteers of America and serving as a puppeteering instructor.

Jack's second imagination-centered story of 1970 was *Mr. Meebles*, also published by Parents' Magazine Press. Mr. Meebles is Donald's imaginary friend, and they have fantastic adventures together, visiting fairy tale lands with dragons, spying on pirates, and outrunning bandits in the Wild West, all illustrated by Jack in large watercolor tableaux. But Donald is growing up, and he begins to find he has less and less time for his friend.

Mr. Meebles starts to wonder where he goes when he's not with Donald, who replies, "Why, nowhere, I guess. . . . You're just an idea, and an idea doesn't exist unless somebody has it." This disturbs Mr. Meebles, who foresees a day when Donald won't think of him at all. Donald eventually writes a note with his friend's name on it to help him remember, but when Mr. Meebles accidentally keeps the note, it allows him to exist without depending on Donald. "Mr. Meebles was only an idea," the narrator tells us. "But the idea was his own now."

As with *The Blah*, Jack didn't take a conventional approach to his resolution. Rather than have Donald realize how much Mr. Meebles means to him and then find a way to keep that part of his childhood alive, Jack allows Mr. Meebles his own agency and freedom. Coming as it did in the midst of a frantic period of creativity for Jack, it's hard not to read this as a metaphor for writing books as a way of remembering and being remembered. Indeed, Donald says, "Whenever I have an idea I want to remember, I write it down." Jack dedicated the book to Alvin Tresselt, without whom Jack likely would never have become a children's author.

Jack's third book of 1970 was an oversized collection of six enduring fairy tales and one lesser-known story (the amusing Norwegian folktale "The Husband Who Tried to Keep House"). Though it bears the title *Jack Kent's Book of Nursery Tales*, Jack didn't write the text. The tales were instead retold by Polly Berrien Berends, an editor at Random House. Jack dedicated the book to her in an allusion to the nursery rhyme, "To Polly, who put the kettle on." (He'd also dedicated *The Grown-Up Day* to Polly; she'd likely been Jack's editor on *Clotilda* and another of his early mentors.)

The text of these retellings was largely straightforward and familiar, but Jack made the stories his own through his visual wit. In "The Little Red Hen," for instance, each lazy animal is doing something unusually funny: the Pig reads a book of mud pie recipes, the Duck floats in the pond on a duck-shaped floaty, and the Cat slathers herself with suntan oil. In "Chicken Little," Henny Penny gives her egg to a "Baby Sitting Service" run by a toad who sits on the egg. And in "Little Red Riding Hood," the Wolf ducks through the forest following a sign that reads, "Shortcut to Grandmother's House."

Jack's illustrations for *Jack Kent's Book of Nursery Tales* were done with a thin pen line and generous watercolor, with multiple pictures per page to enhance the storytelling. Perhaps his most bravura achievement in the book is how he called on his Ferguson Map Company experience to create the large "Map of Storyland" on the endpapers, unifying all of the tales into a single geographical location.

Jack didn't spend *all* of his time in 1970 making books, just *most* of it. In May he was honored along with three other Texas authors at Theta Sigma Phi's 19th annual Matrix Dinner, the dinner June had started back in 1951. That October he served as special guest at the annual Open House and Book Fair at St. Luke's Episcopal School, located in the northern suburbs of San Antonio. It was one of the only school appearances he'd ever make.

Chapter 11

A Cartoonist at Heart (1971–1974)

In the early 1970s, Jack realized he was firmly on the path to a sustainable career in children's books. Though he relished his success, it wasn't easy for Jack to shift his sense of his own identity. Maybe it was the fact that *King Aroo* had started with great promise before becoming financially untenable. Maybe it was that he was getting older, and the rapid transformations of his younger days—from nomad to Texas Jack, from high schooler to working man, from civilian to soldier and back—were no longer so easy to make. But mostly it was the fact that no matter how he had changed other aspects of his life, Jack had always been a cartoonist.

Going all the way back to his choice to create the persona of "Texas Jack," self-perception and identity were something Jack clearly thought about a lot. These themes were a constant presence in *King Aroo* and would be in his children's books as well (*Just Only John* was just the first of many books to address it). When his characters sought out transformation, it was often out of dissatisfaction with their current self. In *King Aroo* this often led the character in question to an identity crisis. In one series of strips, Mathilda, Wanda Witch's assistant, drinks an experimental potion that causes her to change form constantly, so much so that she can't remember what she was to start with. In a 1956 storyline, Yupyop buys a detective kit that includes a disguise. Once he puts it on, his main case becomes trying to find out who he is. In two June 1953 Sunday strips, Charley the Chameleon makes himself look exactly like Wilbur the Mouse, and the pair promptly lose track of who's who.

It seems that Jack tried to use semantics to avoid losing this treasured part of his identity. "I'm flattered when a reviewer calls me an author and an illustrator," he said in a 1977 interview. "I'm still a cartoonist at heart." And while it's true that he would always approach his books from a cartoonist's perspective—and that's arguably a big part of what made his books so appealing—from 1970 on, Jack was demonstrably no longer a professional cartoonist. Eventually he accepted this, keeping his membership in the National Cartoonists' Society but also joining the Authors' Guild and the Authors' League of America. And he would begin to admit, to himself and to others, that his being a children's author was his true calling. Or as he put it, his "destiny."

Jack found that creating children's books certainly wasn't any easier than being a newspaper cartoonist, at least not at first. For the first handful of years of his second career, he worked the same long hours—fifteen hours a day, seven days a week—as he had when he was facing a daily deadline for *King Aroo*. And as with his comic strip, his workaholic tendencies dovetailed with his genuine love for what he was doing.

He'd often circulate over a dozen stories at once to various editors. This also helped mitigate his fear of being rebuffed:

> I would take a rejection out of its sack, see what the editor had to say if anything, check the manuscript over for coffee stains and torn corners, and put it in an envelope to somebody else. I wouldn't reread it to try to find out what they didn't like about it. . . . The editor may have been up too late last night, or had a quarrel with his or her spouse, or have indigestion or whatever, and that would probably result in a negative reaction. If it was the best thing they ever saw on the subject but they already had something in their stable in that particular category, they're not in the market for it.

Circulating multiple proposals at once not only circumnavigated the pain of rejection but made sure Jack would have several projects at different stages of the publication process at once. He held fast to his freelancer's mindset that if he was idle he was not getting paid.

Jack's early manuscribbles zigzagged across the country sometimes six to twelve times before finally finding a home. As the years went on, Jack established relationships with various editors and publishers, and since he didn't have an agent, he would typically accept a contract without negotiation, as long as it seemed reasonable to him. Money wasn't his primary objective, and having multiple books in print simultaneously kept pressure off of any one specific project. He also liked not being beholden to any particular publisher, as it gave him freedom to move on if he felt the publisher hadn't made a decent enough effort to promote one of his earlier books or if an editor was difficult to work with.

• • •

In 1971, Jack would release two books, both with Parents' Magazine Press. *The Wizard of Wallaby Wallow* was yet another book with a great kinship to *King Aroo*. It concerns a wizard who, like Wanda Witch, sometimes loses the labels on his potions and a mouse who, like so many other Kent characters, wishes to be something other than what he is. But unlike in Jack's comic, the transformations in *The Wizard of Wallaby Wallow* don't actually occur. Instead, they all happen in the mouse's imagination before he even ingests the spell. And as he imagines each transformation, he also imagines the downsides, leading him to decide not to take the potion at all. Self-acceptance is a common moral in children's books—it was there in *Just Only John* as well as books like the Theo. LeSieg/Barney Tobey Beginner Book *I Wish That I Had Duck Feet*—but the elegant part of *The Wizard of Wallaby Wallow* is that the book doesn't end there. The mouse goes to return his unused potion, and the Wizard is so delighted that his spell worked (even if not in the way it was designed) that he ends up changing his whole business practice and helping everyone in town find self-acceptance when they need it.

Jack's humorous wordsmithing is on full display, such as when the wizard "swears" ("Oh, geese fleece") or when the narrator tells us, "Work was not one of the mouse's favorite activities." And then there's the wry moral: "Being me has problems," the mouse muses, "but at least I know what they are."

The Fat Cat, also published in 1971, would turn out to be one of Jack's most beloved and memorable books, and it remains in print more than fifty years later. Told in a cumulative style (where sentences repeat, with new information added on each page), it's the story of a cat with an increasingly voracious appetite. The traditional folktale—variations of which have been recorded in countries as diverse as India, Sweden, and Czechia—had appeared as a children's book just a year before, in Jeanne B. Hardendorff and Emily McCully's *Slip, Slop, Gobble*. Jack's version was a translation of a Danish version, "Den Tykke Kat," from a book by Elias Berdsdorff called *Danish: An Elementary Grammar and Reader* (1958, Cambridge University Press). Jack, of course, had taken up the study of Danish in tribute to June's roots and the Kents had become quite friendly with her cousins Hugo and Bodil Christiansen, who made their home in Kolding, Denmark.

As with *Jack Kent's Book of Nursery Tales*, much of the power of Jack's version of the story is the marriage of the dark and disturbing material so common to fairy and folktales with jolly lighthearted illustrations. In *The Fat Cat*, the horror comes not only from the fact that the cat gobbles up several citizens of the town and becomes increasingly grotesquely large but from it ending with him having his stomach cut open with an ax and everyone spilling out fully alive. The picture of the latter features most of the characters either jubilant or just slightly dazed by the experience; and of the cat we only see upended feet. Further, Jack extends the story by adding a final illustration of the woodcutter placing bandages on the now-small cat's stomach.

The lesson of the story—that greed and gluttony are harmful—is only implied, not stated outright. Surely, however, given his political views, Jack relished the double meaning of the term "fat cat" as being a rich, greedy person.

In 1976 and 1977, Jack made two attempts to create a sequel to *The Fat Cat*, creating full manuscribbles for both stories. The first, titled *The Fat Cat's Kitten Caboodle*, finds the cat's nephews and niece—Smarty Cat, Fraidy Cat, and Copy Cat—visiting their uncle, who is inexplicably still fat. The story follows their quest to get a fruit from a Foofaw tree in order to shrink him back to his normal size. To do this, they have to overcome a vicious creature called the Grizzlegrump.

A page from the "manuscribble" for *The Fat Cat's Kitten Caboodle*, ca. mid-1970s. Jack Kent Papers. Kerlan Collection, Children's Literature Research Collections, University of Minnesota Libraries, Minneapolis. Courtesy of Jack Kent Jr. and the Kerlan Collection.

In *The Fat Cat and the Terrible Awful Grizzlegrump,* Fat Cat is being visited by his *five* nieces and nephews, each of whom has a special power. One can turn into other shapes, one can stretch his neck, one can run fast, one is super strong, and one can make things disappear. But one by one each kitten—done in by its own hubris—gets eaten by the terrible awful Grizzlegrump. The cat then eats the Grizzlegrump, making him fat again, which leads to a humorous misunderstanding with the woodcutter who'd saved him in the first book.

The two have obvious overlaps in story elements, and each one has its charms. The usual Kentian wit is present in *The Fat Cat's Kitten Caboodle* in lines such as "The eldest was the Smarty Cat. For every question he had at least three answers, one of which was sometimes right." And it has a funny ending, with the whole group sitting down to wait six years for the Foofaw seed to grow into a Foofaw tree. *The Fat Cat and the Terrible Awful Grizzlegrump* has a strong structure, and the kittens' powers give Jack a lot to work with visually. Their overconfidence about their powers lends a clear but subtle moral

A page from the "manuscribble" for *The Fat Cat and the Terrible Awful Grizzlegrump*, ca. mid-1970s. Jack Kent Papers. Kerlan Collection, Children's Literature Research Collections, University of Minnesota Libraries, Minneapolis. Courtesy of Jack Kent Jr. and the Kerlan Collection.

about the danger of making assumptions, which is underscored by the woodcutter's misunderstanding of the Fat Cat's intentions.

But it's apparent why neither book found a publisher. *Kitten Caboodle* is too light on plot, and its whole conceit ignores the fact that the cat was no longer fat at the end of the original book. The *Terrible Awful Grizzlegrump* has an ending that feels perfunctory and unsatisfying. With a strong final punch line or humorously stated lesson, the book might have been a worthy addition to his oeuvre.

• • •

Traditional tales figured prominently in Jack's work in the early 1970s. He created two volumes worth of adaptations of Aesop's Fables for Parents' Magazine Press, *Jack Kent's Book of Fables* and *More Fables of Aesop*. The first was released in 1972, and the second in 1974. In *King Aroo*, Jack had played around with Aesop on at least three occasions.

King Aroo, November 3, 1955. Courtesy of Jack Kent Jr.

In addition to the 1951 strip in which the hare claims the story's facts were misreported, there's a 1955 strip in which the dog seeing his reflection in the water is in truth another dog and a 1957 one in which a fox actually gets the grapes only to find that they actually *are* sour.

Jack's tellings of those morality tales (and twenty-four others) in these two volumes are much more straightforward and faithful to the originals than his *King Aroo* takeoffs. Jack drew from V. S. Vernon Jones's 1916 versions of the stories, though he admits in the brief preface that he interpreted them "freely." And as with his other work on fairy and folktales, a lot of Jack's inventiveness comes in the drawings rather than the text. For instance, in "The Town Mouse and the Country Mouse," the town mouse's feast includes grape soda and a TV dinner. And in "The Fox and the Grapes," the fox tries to get at the grapes by standing on a sign that reads "Do not pick the grapes." And the sleeping lion in "The Lion and the Mouse" is pictured with a nightcap and nightshirt in a comfy bed with an alarm clock on the side table.

Also published in 1972 was *Dooly and the Snortsnoot*, the story of an undersized young giant who believes that he will never grow. He decides to compensate by becoming frightening and important, because "when you feel important, you feel big." But he finds that yelling, "Fee Fi Fo Fum!" at dogs and other children doesn't have the desired effect. The children treat it like a game and try to give him tips on doing it more authentically. When the dragon-cat Snortsnoot arrives and begins terrorizing everyone in the town, Dooly finds the determination to be brave and confront the creature. Only then does he start to grow. In part it's a story about arriving at maturity—"I think I just grew up because it was time to" Dooly concludes—yet that maturity brings the realization that power doesn't come from intimidating others but from being courageous in the face of your fears.

In addition to the seven books he released in 1970, 1971, and 1972, Jack made frequent contributions to *Humpty Dumpty's Magazine*. Between January 1970 and July 1972, Jack placed approximately fifteen stories in the magazine (four of those bearing his art on the cover, as well). Three of the stories—"Mr. Meebles," "The Wonderful Magic Spell," and "Aesop's Fables"—were taken from his books, but the rest never appeared anywhere else. It was an impressive burst of creativity in a short period of time.

The stories were usually around seven pages long, with four or five illustrations. Four of them—all featuring the same brother and sister pair—were more like picture books, with limited text and illustrations on each page. The artwork in all of them is of a piece, a thick ink line with a single flat color on each page providing backgrounds and/or patterns.

A few of the stories took their cues from ideas Jack had started to explore in *King Aroo*. "Oscar" (Jan. 1970) is about an ostrich who ends up with his head in a bucket of sand, echoing a June 1964 strip. "King Norton the Nasty" (Jan. 1972), which features a monarch who expresses his emotions through different masks, is similar to a 1960 storyline. And "Lovely Day" (Feb. 1970) is about a weatherman who longs to predict something other than "fair and mild" and goes on a trip to find other sorts of weather. A running joke in *King Aroo* was that the weather was controlled by the weatherman.

There were cute and sweet tales, such as "Toggle" (1970), which is about "a long dog with a short memory," and "The Runaway" (1971), featuring a boy who doesn't appreciate his home until he meets a homeless dog. In "Let's Be Frogs" (1972), two children enjoy pretending to be frogs until they remember that frogs eat flies.

Other stories reached for the profound. "The Lonely Tree" (Apr. 1970) finds a loving, interconnected community of animals and plants forming around a forlorn tree. In "The Butterfly" (1971), a boy and a girl chase and capture a butterfly. As they admire it in a jar, they begin to picture themselves in jars and then decide to release their prize.

• • •

A page from "The Butterfly," which appeared in Humpty Dumpty's Magazine, October 1971. Courtesy of Jack Kent Jr.

The year 1973 marked another shift in the Kent household. June retired from the *San Antonio Express*, and Jack Jr. graduated from high school and headed off to college at Rice University in Houston to study architecture. Jack began using Jack Jr.'s room for a studio, the first time in his career he had a separate area to work.

And that was good, because his career was blossoming. Not only were his books selling well, they were being issued in paperback and included in increasingly popular book clubs, such as Scholastic and Weekly Reader. They were also being translated into other languages, something that made Jack very happy. He hadn't lost his love for studying languages and had added Dutch, Afrikaans, and Hebrew

Photo of Jack with many translations of his children's books, taken by Robert McLeroy for the San Antonio Express-News in 1980. Courtesy of Robert McLeroy/*San Antonio Express-News*/ZUMA Press.

to the list of languages he had a "nodding acquaintance" with (he also liked to joke that he was still working on English). So seeing his books in other languages was a great thrill. It also gave him a chance to practice his reading skills.

> I was kind of intrigued in one instance where the same story was translated into Danish and Swedish. I was comparing the two. The Swedish told the story and that was it. The Danish picked up the fillips that I had put in, and it was a much lighter telling than the other. I don't say that's the way Swedes look at things, but that particular one did!

Jack released two books in 1973, *Mrs. Mooley* and *Jack Kent's Twelve Days of Christmas*. *Mrs. Mooley*, published by Golden Press, is the second of his children's books to use characters and a storyline from *King Aroo*. But unlike in *Mr. Elephant's Birthday Party*, both are changed significantly. Mrs. Mooley first appeared in *King Aroo* in 1951 as a grandmotherly cow whose moon-jumping days are behind her. In an extended April 1954 storyline, she decides to try it again and ends up with her housedress caught on the point of the crescent moon.

In the book version, Mrs. Mooley is a young cow, and she becomes inspired to attempt to jump over the moon when she happens across "Hey Diddle Diddle" in a book of nursery rhymes (in a clever touch, the book is Alice and Martin Provensen's 1948 *The Giant Golden Mother Goose*, which was also published by Golden Press). And it's not a little dog that laughs at the notion but a whole barnyard full of animals. Undeterred, she keeps trying, repeating the mantra, "All it takes is determination . . . and a little practice." This was a clear expression of two of Jack's central beliefs: that you were only limited by the boundaries you put on yourself or let others put on you.

In the end, Mrs. Mooley achieves her impossible task but, as with the *King Aroo* gang, the barnyard animals—and Mrs. Mooley herself—are all too naïve to realize it only happened because the moon has sunk so low on the horizon. Even so, it's worth noting that Mrs. Mooley's final jump is her highest yet. The book's first edition was oversized (10" by 12"), and Jack loosened his ink line considerably, nearly to the squiggly levels of illustrators such as William Steig and Quentin Blake. The watercolors are thick and bold.

His second book of 1973 was *Jack Kent's Twelve Days of Christmas*, yet another Parents' Magazine Press publication. It was Jack's most bravura illustrative work up to that point. Though the text is just the lyrics to the familiar yule song, it's Jack's literal interpretation of them in the pictures that moves it into the realm of genius. Rather than simply illustrate the number and type of gifts from each day, Jack actually depicts the cumulative effect. So the true love (in this case a top-hatted boy) doesn't just bring the narrator (a girl with a Santa cap) a partridge in a pear tree on the first day, but one on every subsequent day as well. And two turtledoves each day, and three French hens, and so on, in addition to the new item. This means, of course, that by the end Jack has drawn 364 different items. And the girl, who has become increasingly alarmed by her true love's exuberance and generosity, has run off to hide.

The book's dedication page featured a pear tree with a tag labeled, "To Florence." This was Florence Rosengren of Rosengren's Books.

Her husband, Frank, had retired from the store in 1942 and passed away in 1949, but Florence was going strong. The store had endured a couple of moves and had settled into a location in the Crockett Hotel behind the Alamo. Florence was known to champion local writers, but only if she liked their work. She liked Jack's work and along with Sue Shields, who managed the children's department, featured his books prominently in the store. Whenever Jack released a new book, the store held an autograph party with sherry, cheese, coffee, and cookies. Jack would not only sign books but often add a sketch. Since he didn't do book tours, this and an occasional interview were often the extent of his promotional efforts.

It wasn't just book tours that Jack eschewed. For all of their love of travel, Jack and June would rarely venture far from home in the 1970s. One major exception was a weeklong trip to Russia in the fall of 1974. While there, they saw an opera and went to a variety show ("Vaudeville is alive and marvelous in Russia," they reported) in Leningrad and attended both a ballet and a circus on ice in Moscow. They had their favorite meal of the trip at a Uzbekistani restaurant. It would be Jack and June's last significant trip together.

Chapter 12

Fringe Benefits (1975–1979)

As he entered his midfifties, Jack found himself less and less inclined to venture very far from home. He may not have been diagnosed as having social anxiety disorder or agoraphobia, but Jack was no longer comfortable being around big groups or around people he hadn't met before. Some of this came from contentment; the once outgoing and gregarious "Texas Jack" preferred being in the house reading, working, or gardening, with only June or his mother for company.

The other part of it came from necessity: it was a full-time job and more to keep up with deadlines while also serving as his own agent and business manager. This was compounded by the fact that Jack was taking on more work than he ever had before, partially because, in addition to writing and drawing his own books, he'd begun illustrating other authors' books.

This had kicked off with Ruth Belov Gross's 1974 retelling of the Brothers Grimm story "Town Musicians of Bremen," here titled *The Bremen Town Musicians*. Jack's character designs are as cute and expressive as ever, and his staging is wonderful, but mostly this is a very straightforward illustration job without the visual extensions and jokes he often gave his own stories.

Jack found he enjoyed illustrating books for other authors immensely. It allowed him to focus on his favorite part of the process of making a book. "I write the words so I can draw the pictures," he once remarked. But it wasn't always easy: "In a few instances," he recalled, "when I saw the manuscript I was horrified, but I took it as a challenge—can I make something of this?"

Two books Jack illustrated in 1975 show the different ways he approached the challenge of bringing a manuscript to life: Carla Stevens's *How to Make Possum's Honey Bread* (Seabury Press) and Sarah E. Barchas's *I Was Walking Down the Road* (Scholastic). The former is essentially a recipe told in story form and very well may have "horrified" Jack on his first read through in terms of finding a way to illustrate it. Even if it wasn't, *How to Make Possum's Honey Bread* is definitely not one of Jack's more inspired efforts. The very loose pen line and generic character designs, along with an uncharacteristic sloppiness on the labels of the flour, salt, etc. (this from the cartoonist whose calligraphy was such a strong element of his skill set), seem to indicate a lack of engagement, time, or both.

By great contrast, his work on *I Was Walking Down the Road* was a clinic on how text and pictures can work together in harmony to enhance one another. Barchas, an elementary school librarian from Arizona, took her idea for a story about a girl who collects animals from her own childhood love of pets and from her professional experience of recognizing the need for more books that were accessible to beginning readers. She deliberately wrote *I Was Walking Down the Road* using both rhyme and repetition to help make the text predictable, but what Barchas didn't foresee was how having Jack assigned to illustrate her book would make it even more new-reader friendly.

The pattern in the book is simple: the girl is doing an activity, sees an animal, catches it, and puts it in a cage. Likely recognizing that depicting this literally would become monotonous, Jack turned each episode into a ministory of its own. So once the girl gets the frog into its cage, Jack's pictures show it jumping away, cage and all, until she sits on top of it. And when she catches the snake, her little dog is terrified until the snake is securely in the cage and then makes a big show of toughness and walks away feeling very satisfied. These little stories within the story not only are uniformly funny but give the young reader more to engage with and get excited about.

Some of the stories Jack wrote himself in 1974 and 1975 also showed a fascination with early reading principles. Jack didn't have any great love for controlled vocabulary early reader children's books such as the Dick and Jane primers, calling them "ridiculous." (In a Feb. 1952 *King Aroo* Sunday strip, Abou Ben Riley reads King Aroo's mind and declares him to be the elementary type: "I see the cat. The cat sees me. The cat sees the rat. I see the rat. The rat sees the cat. The rat sees. . . .") He thought that language was too important to limit and that children should be exposed to lots of different words.

But that didn't mean he couldn't address early readers in other ways. *Jack Kent's Hop, Skip and Jump Book* (1974, Random House) was essentially a vocabulary book consisting of various scenes labeled with applicable nouns and verbs, much in the manner of Richard Scarry's *Best Word Book Ever*. Children cavort through home, school, and city, and the book is full of little visual vignettes, such as the boy who has spilled his paint cup in the classroom scene or the mother closing the door with relief after a visit from a gang of children.

In terms of the early reading continuum, Jack went a step even further backward with *The Egg Book*, published by Macmillan in 1975. The story of a hen looking for an egg to hatch contains no text at all, catering to prereaders who learn instinctually to "read the pictures." The concept for the book had come from the head of Macmillan's children's books, Susan Hirschman, who up to that point had politely refused every single book pitch Jack sent her. Her rejections had become so predictable that Jack began to take it as a challenge to find an idea she'd accept.

Since the illustrations were the story, Jack made them appropriately bold. He employed a thick brush line for the first time in many years, and the watercolor work is akin to that of *Mrs. Mooley*: bright, saturated, and warm. Jack expertly depicted his heroine's wide range of emotions, perhaps none better than her initial dismissiveness toward the egg she laid herself.

The year 1975 also saw the publication of one of Jack's most enduring and well-loved books. *There's No Such Thing as a Dragon* is about a boy named Billy Bixbee who wakes up one morning to find a dragon "about the size of a kitten" sitting on the end of his bed. He acknowledges the dragon with a pat on the head, but when his mother tells him there's no such thing as a dragon, he reluctantly begins to ignore the creature. Even as it begins to grow larger and larger, both Billy and his mother pretend the dragon isn't there. Soon it's so big, it's no longer possible to ignore.

102 Fringe Benefits (1975–1979)

Again and again Jack's work—both in children's books and earlier in *King Aroo*—explored the intersection of imagination and reality. *The Blah* and *The Wizard of Wallaby Wallow* were both about the power of imagination to help us better face reality. And *Mr. Meebles* focused on how our ideas take on lives of their own, but *There's No Such Thing as a Dragon* looks at what happens to ideas and realities that we try to ignore. The more Billy and his mother deny the dragon, the bigger it gets and the more of a destructive force it becomes.

In one way this is a story that plays on the old saying about avoiding obvious problems, turning "the elephant in the room" into "the dragon in the room." But, as in *Clotilda*, there's also a message about the power and reward of acknowledging the magical things that are all around us. Once Billy admits that the dragon does exist, giving it another pat on the head, the dragon shrinks back down to kitten size. At this point even Billy's mom embraces the dragon, letting it fall asleep in her lap.

In *King Aroo*, there are multiple instances of creatures (sea serpents, ghosts, dodo birds) who are told they don't exist. Jack often used these scenarios out of his devotion to absurdity—and really what's more absurd than a sea serpent in the castle moat arguing against his very existence? And though *There's No Such Thing as a Dragon* can be read on a deeper level, Jack still has fun with the absurdity of the concept. The story is full of droll moments, such as when the dragon gets on the table and Billy's mother has no recourse: "She had already said there was no such thing as a dragon. And if there's no such thing, you can't tell it to get down off the table." Or after the dragon has run off with the house on his back, and the text tells us, "When Mr. Bixbee came home for lunch, the first thing he noticed was that the house was gone."

• • •

In November 1975 Jack's work was included in an exhibition called "Children's Book Art: An Exhibition of Art of Children's Literature" at the Contemporary Arts Museum in Houston. His work appeared alongside a who's who of kids' book illustrators: Edward Gorey, Trina Schart Hyman, Margot Zemach, Arnold Lobel, José Aruego and Arianne Dewey, and James Marshall. In the program, Jack wrote that

Fringe Benefits (1975–1979)

King Aroo, December 9, 1956. Courtesy of Jack Kent Jr.

he hoped his books would make fellow book lovers out of his young readers then added, "While that is the vaunted purpose, it must be confessed that I do what I do because I like doing it. All else is fringe benefit."

It's no surprise then that the second half of the 1970s was Jack's most prolific time in children's books. He published an astonishing twenty-eight books between 1975 and 1979. A large reason for his productivity was a drastic increase in the number of books he illustrated for other authors. When it came to his own books, Jack was constantly the pursuer, relentlessly looking to place them with a publisher. It was the opposite when it came to illustrating for others. Though he enjoyed illustration work, he never sought it out, waiting instead for editors to offer. And offer they did.

In the process of establishing his career in children's books, Jack had formed relationships with several editors and publishers, so much of his illustration work was done for publishers he had worked with previously. Scholastic continued to be his most frequent destination. Jack did five books for the publisher in the late 1970s alone: *Freya*

Littledale's *Seven at One Blow* (1976), Rita Goldman Gelman's *Why Can't I Fly?* and *More Spaghetti, I Say!* (1976 and 1977), Ruth Belov Gross's *The Emperor's New Clothes* (1977), and Sarah Barchas's *Janie and the Giant* (1978).

But there was a smattering of other publishers, too. For Random House he did the postcard book *Tiny and Tony* (1977). Over at Parents' Magazine Press, Jack illustrated Jane Yolen's *The Simple Prince* (1978). For Atheneum it was Beatrice Schenk de Regniers's *Laura's Story* (1979). And for Doubleday he did Bonnie Bishop's *No One Noticed Ralph* and *Ralph Rides Away* (both 1979).

Jack used his illustration assignments to experiment with his style and mediums. Not only did it keep things interesting for him, it allowed him to best serve the story. So for the early readers *Why Can't I Fly?* and *More Spaghetti, I Say!* he employed a thin ink line, simple, minimal backgrounds, and spare use of bright, flat colors. For the fairy tale *Seven at One Blow* (a retelling of "The Brave Little Tailor"), he used thick brushwork, lush watercolors, and detailed settings. In *Janie and the Giant* he demonstrated the giant's power and size with only black and brown, relying on the two colors—rather than his line work—to define shape and form.

Sometimes Jack approached his illustration work in a very straightforward way, depicting the text more or less literally. But other times he extended the story, throwing in visual jokes and gags that went beyond the text. For the postcards in *Tiny and Tony*, Jack had fun with the boilerplate greeting card messages such as "We go well together" (as they share a skateboard), "Happy birthday" (Tony skis down Tiny's birthday sundae), and "Have a nice trip" (Tiny throws a paper airplane with Tony aboard). *Janie and the Giant* gave Jack a chance to put his sense of humor into the story. For a scene where Janie and the giant compete to see who can stretch taller, Jack drew the giant so tall that most of his body is off the page, while little Janie struggles on her tiptoes.

• • •

The second half of the 1970s also found Jack combining his two careers. *I Was Walking Down the Road* marked the first time Jack experimented with bringing his experience in sequential comic strips into his children's book work, and he continued and furthered that with *Jack Kent's Merry Mother Goose* (1977), *The Funny Book* (1977), and *Cindy Lou and the Witch's Dog* (1978).

In *Jack Kent's Merry Mother Goose*, published by Random House, Jack presents familiar nursery rhymes in comic strip style, both in humor and form (some even have panel boxes). The rhymes themselves are presented unaltered, but Jack's pictures often reinterpret the text. For example, we learn that Old Mother Hubbard's cupboard is bare because all of the dishes fell out when she opened the doors. Little Jumping Joan is all alone because she jumped on (and broke) all of her friends' toys. And Little Miss Muffet was actually the victim of a prank, as the arachnid that came down beside her was just a plastic spider dangling on a string. All of this was of a piece with the irreverent way Jack treated nursery rhymes in *King Aroo*.

Jack's other visual revisions don't change the meaning of the rhymes as much as add a bit of fun to them. So the king hides under his table once the four and twenty blackbirds emerge from the pie, Little Jack Horner dribbles pie filling all over the carpet, and Jack Be Nimble's pants catch fire when he jumps over the candlestick. Visually this is one of Jack's most eye-catching and eye-pleasing works, the oversized pages showing off a thin, slightly wobbly but careful ink line and warm, full color. One page features seven different rhymes, all woven together through Jack's interconnected pictures.

The Funny Book, published by Golden Books, is a unique hybrid of a comic collection and joke book. It's filled with wordless gag cartoons from Jack's freelance days (at least one of the gags—a baton twirler whose arm becomes a corkscrew—Jack submitted to *Mad* in the 1960s). To give the book a semblance of coherence, many of the cartoons feature a king and his attendant; indeed, the book's working title was *The Royal Funny Book*. But somewhat incongruously mixed in are question-and-answer jokes about cows, sheep, knights, and ghosts. There are also anecdotes and dialogues, such as:

Ben: It's unpossible!
Katy: You mean impossible, don't you?
Ben: I mean it can't be did!

Finally, *Cindy Lou and the Witch's Dog*, published by Random House, is Jack most comic strip-indebted children's book. Told using panels, sound effects, and dialogue balloons (originally intended to be hand lettered by Jack, but typeset in the final book), it revisits ideas from *King Aroo*, namely the escapades of George the Goblin and Wanda Witch's assistant Mathilda. Like George, the witch's dog in this story—Prince—changes shape whenever he hiccups. Cindy Lou joins Prince in several funny misadventures, including one that, as happened to Mathilda in *King Aroo*, starts at a cat show and ends with a multitude of cats stuck in a single tree. Unlike Jack's other tales of transformation, this one doesn't have any deeper theme or moral. Instead it's a lighthearted romp with a clever twist ending (Prince is cured of his hiccups but then starts sneezing, setting off a new round of transformations).

• • •

Jack's work, from *King Aroo* to his children's books, showed a consistent love of fairy and folktales. Not only did Jack create his own folktale in the late 1970s (1978's O. Henry-indebted *Socks for Supper*), he continued to present his own versions of traditional tales.

In 1976 and 1979 he released two sequels to *Jack Kent's Book of Nursery Tales*. *Jack Kent's Happy Ever After Book* and *Jack Kent's Hokus Pokus Bedtime Book* featured ten more fairy tales in oversized volumes, including "Beauty and the Beast," "Puss In Boots," and "Jack and the Beanstalk."

This time Jack wrote the text himself, keeping it mostly traditional but inserting a wry line here and there (such as "They agreed to do what he said because, coming from a cat in boots, the order somehow seemed important" and "'People who are truly stupid,' Beauty assured him, 'are too stupid to know it.'"). The pictures in both books were done in a thin ink line and bright watercolors and provide several humorous extensions from the text. There's the Beast eating out of a dog dish with his name on it, Snow White taking a nap lying across the beds of all seven dwarves, and a "Just Married" sign hanging on the back of the horse that Sleeping Beauty and the Prince ride away on.

Hoddy Doddy was a collection of three humorous Danish folk-tales—"The Lobster," "The Clock," and "The Patriot." Besides their common origin, all three stories feature characters who are foolish in some way (one of the definitions of a "hoddy doddy" is "fool"). The book *Hoddy Doddy* was significant because it represented only the second time Jack was able to land a contract with his friend Susan Hirschman and the first time that it was with his own story idea. The editor had left Macmillan and started her own imprint at William Morris, Greenwillow.

Jack had written to her immediately upon hearing the news in early 1975, saying, "I want on your list. . . . It wouldn't give Greenwillow any prestige, but it sure would make me happy." *Hoddy Doddy* fulfilled that wish. This pleased not only Jack but Susan as well. After having to reject him so many times, Susan and her team were thrilled to be able to finally say, "Yes!" Jack would also illustrate Richard J. Margolis's *Big Bear, Spare That Tree* for the publisher in 1980. Susan found Jack to be a pleasure to work with. She says, "He was talented and not full of himself—a rare combination."

Chapter 13

No Great Genius (1980–1983)

A new decade brought two landmark events to the lives of the Kent family. On the happy side, Jack Jr. graduated from Rice University and landed a position at an architecture firm in Houston. Jack was exceedingly proud. In a self-written biography for the National Cartoonist's Society, he proclaimed, "My son is a genius." On the sad side, the family dachshund, Toggle, died at the age of eighteen. The house was empty without its monarch.

What remained the same was the ongoing parade of children's book projects marching across Jack's desk and his long work hours devoted to them. The only real difference professionally was a drastic reduction in the number of books he did for other authors. The ones that he did do, however, he put an extraordinary amount of care and effort into.

Ruth Belov Gross's nonfiction *If You Grew Up with George Washington* (Scholastic, 1982) featured over fifty individual pictures, not full color, but with the linework and ink wash printed in red-violet. In 1979 Jack had created a 26-frame educational filmstrip titled *How Did They Get from Here to There When George Washington Was Young?* For that project, Jack clearly did his research on settings and costumes, and that work translated over to *If You Grew Up with George Washington*. In both cases, he managed to marry his humor to historical accuracy, for example in a picture of a large pile of malformed horseshoes surrounding an apprentice farrier and of a small dog's frightened reaction to the masks women wore to protect their faces from the sun.

Original art from the Scholastic filmstrip *How Did They Get from Here to There in George Washington's Time?*, 1979. Jack Kent Papers. Kerlan Collection, Children's Literature Research Collections, University of Minnesota Libraries, Minneapolis. Courtesy of Jack Kent Jr. and the Kerlan Collection.

Jack also worked with Gross on *The Girl Who Wouldn't Get Married* (Four Winds, 1983). Based on the Norwegian story "The Squire's Bride," it's a funny book enhanced greatly by Jack's artwork. It wasn't unusual for Jack to extend a story through his artwork, but this book marked the first and only time that he added hand-lettered dialogue and sound effects to many of his drawings. None of the dialogue repeats the text but, instead, it adds to and deepens the story. Judging by a note Ruth Belov Gross sent to Jack, this both surprised and delighted her. The drawings themselves are perhaps the most delicate of Jack's to ever see print, done with a slightly shaky thin line and careful watercolors.

· · ·

Even fifteen years into his children's book career, Jack was still trying new things. In the 1970s he'd done some unconventional projects for Scholastic, including a small foldout book illustrating the lyrics to

"Deck the Halls" and *The Animobile Book*, a build-it-yourself hanging mobile depicting various animals and their babies. In the eighties, he did *Jack Kent's Sticker Fun Drawing Book* (1981), which came with sheets of brightly colored stickers in various geometric shapes, and *Jack Kent's Valentine Sticker Book* (1982), which contained twenty-two tear-out valentines and four sheets of stickers with animals and message hearts (the funniest of which reads, "I love you anyway").

And then, in the spring of 1982, Jack was invited by President Ronald Reagan's administration to decorate three wooden eggs for the annual White House Easter Egg Roll. The event had a long history dating back to the presidency of Rutherford B. Hayes in the 1870s, but this was just the second time that artists were invited to paint eggs. After being used in the roll, the eggs would be displayed in the Smithsonian Institute in Washington, DC. Jack was flattered, though a bit baffled as to how he came to the attention of the president's office. Turns out, White House Visitors' Office director Carol McCain said staff had seen his children's books and thought he would make a good representative from the Southwest. Jack's eggs had paintings of King Aroo and Round Robin and were briefly displayed along with the other artists' eggs at the Smithsonian.

• • •

You'd think that coming to the attention of a US president would convince Jack that he had "made it" as a children's book author. But even in the face of this and many other validations, Jack couldn't shake the specter of failure. Jack's experiences—his constant childhood moves, dropping out of high school, fighting in World War II, his divorce, the demise of *King Aroo*—left him with an underlying insecurity and a nagging feeling that he wasn't reaching full potential.

Whether consciously or not, Jack used his books to open up about his insecurities and detail his constant battle for self-acceptance, and he did so in funny, heartfelt, and profound ways. In book after book, Jack's characters are looking to feel valued and valuable, and that desire causes them to seek out new homes and new identities. This pattern continued into the last creations of Jack's career as a children's author: books that addressed his feelings about his lack of education, the sting of rejection, the loneliness of going unnoticed, and the value of self-love.

Upon first glance *Silly Goose* (Prentice Hall, 1983) seems like, as *School Library Journal* put it, a "nonsensical romp." But underlying that is a message about didacticism that speaks directly to Jack's shame about never having earned his high school diploma. The story concerns a sweater-clad goose who keeps warning a jogging fox about impending danger. But the fox dismisses the goose's warnings because she gets the details wrong, such as when she mistakes a falling *oak* tree for a falling *elm* tree and labels an attacking crocodile as an alligator. This of course leads the fox into great trouble, but each time the goose saves him. If this were an Aesop's fable, the moral would be "One must learn to tell the forest from the trees." The message seems to be that an education without practical experience doesn't amount to much.

While Jack highly valued learning, he seems to have been more ambivalent about schools and classrooms. He liked to say, with a combination of self-deprecation and defiance, that his lack of education "explains a lot but excuses nothing." The fact that he chose not to finish his diploma or go to college on the GI Bill after his stint in the Army shows that perhaps there was more than just economic necessity behind his decision to leave school.

This ambivalence arises several times in *King Aroo*, too. The strips that address education come at it from a few different angles, at times seeming dismissive, at others extolling its virtues. A 1951 Sunday strip is probably closest overall to Jack's true feelings. Here, Mr. Pennipost tells a story about two Dalmatians, one who studied hard and became "lord high coach dog" and the other who spent his school days writing "puppy-love doggerel" and became a firehouse dog. When Mr. Pennipost is about to conclude that the latter dog has led a more interesting and leisurely life than the former, a mother bird dragging her reluctant offspring to school interrupts him: "Exceptions prove the rule!" she huffs.

The 1971 *Humpty Dumpty's Magazine* story "All the Answers" also took on the topic. It finds King Doogil jealous because his rival, King Bilbi, is smarter than him ("He said so himself"). So he sets off to get the answers to every question there is, in the process realizing that

Jack's contribution to *A Private Gem in a Public Setting: An Original Commentary on Education by Some of America's Leading Cartoonists*, a book created to benefit the New College Foundation in Sarasota, Florida, 1978. Courtesy of Jack Kent Jr.

he needs the questions first, and finds himself so wrapped up in his search that he no longer cares about how smart King Bilbi is. As with *Silly Goose*, this was Jack's way of reminding himself that he wasn't "less than" for his lack of education.

Jack's feelings about his lack of education manifested in the way he viewed his books, too. He held himself and his work to a very high standard. And despite his successes—as seen in his receiving mountains of admiring letters from children and teachers and the occasional accolade (a 1976 Arts and Letters Award from the Friends of San Antonio Public Library, for instance)—he seemed almost apologetic for the fact that his books weren't regarded as serious, deep, or challenging.

He said in a 1985 interview, "I'm no great genius in any of the categories involved here—writing or illustrating or otherwise—but the books have been successful. I can only explain it by the fact that there is a market for the type of whimsy, humor, or whatever it is I purvey."

This was another manifestation of his traumatic life experiences. According to Jack Jr., Jack's survivor guilt from his war experiences caused him to place extremely high expectations on himself and to be very hard on himself when he felt he fell short. He felt an obligation to honor his fallen friends by doing work that would make an impact on the world. So there was an irrational but genuine shame about the fact that he took such great pleasure in his work, in writing stories and drawing pictures that amused him. More than once he labeled himself "selfish" for making a living doing something he loved.

It didn't help that Jack never reached a point where he was immune to criticism and rejection from both sides of creating his books and that this reopened wounds from the way that *King Aroo* had risen and fallen. At the behest of editors, Jack often had to make late-stage changes to work that was essentially finished. This involved not just changing a word or two of text but sometimes rewriting and redrawing entire sequences that were already inked and colored and ready for print. He was unfailingly gracious and accommodating about these requests, partly because he felt future work depended on it and partly because his ego was so underinflated.

There were also scores of rejections. Greenwillow's Susan Hirschman vetoed idea after idea. In 1979, after a year and a half of back-and-forth and revisions, she put the kibosh on a book that would have compiled new versions of "Toggle" and "The Runaway" from *Humpty Dumpty's Magazine* along with a third dog story (Jack suggested *Waggish Dog Tales* or *Puppy Dog Tales* as titles). She said "no" to at least seven more of Jack's ideas in 1983 and 1984 alone, including books with tantalizing titles such as *The Other Side of Sundown* and *Alphabugabet*. Jack was discouraged but never dissuaded: "I'm disgusted with me!" he wrote to Hirschman. "I just can't seem to get on your frequency. Needless to say, I will keep on trying."

Reviews were also difficult. Though he did get the occasional rave, the published appraisals of his books were typically laden with backhanded compliments. Take Kirkus's summation of *The Egg Book* as having "bright, simply designed pages that make this look better than many of Kent's picture books." They also wrote of *Jack Kent's*

Happy Ever After Book, "We have to admit that Kent has a talent for this sort of lowbrow comedy." In the *New York Times, Tuck Everlasting* author Natalie Babbitt wrote of *Jack Kent's Merry Mother Goose*, "The volume is genuinely good-hearted, but it somehow manages also to be TV vulgar—which is unfortunate." *School Library Journal* wrote of *The Scribble Monster*, "Kent's cute cartoons and situation (hardly a plot) fail to carry even 32 wordless pages." And these weren't isolated incidents; the majority of Jack's reviews contained similar sentiments.

• • •

Jack couldn't help feeling undervalued, but he put those feelings into his work. Jack had been mining this territory since *King Aroo* (see the "I'm miserable being nobody" strip in Chapter 8) and the 1969 *Mad Magazine* piece "You Know You're Really a Nobody When. . . ". The *Humpty Dumpty's Magazine* story "Nobody" (1971) and the 1979 book *Floyd the Tiniest Elephant* (Doubleday, 1979) also featured characters searching for a place where they're noticed and appreciated. When this type of story is for adults, it's often labeled as neurotic, but as a children's story, it serves as validation for feelings of being small and easily overlooked.

In his children's books, Jack most often addressed self-dissatisfaction through stories of transformation. As Jack Jr. points out, transformation was the motif of Jack's own life: "Rudolf Artur Zurawski becoming Ralph Arthur Kent on the eve of his transfer from Iowa to Texas; the family reinventing itself in new jobs and new cities; Daddy of course reinventing himself from cartoonist to children's author." Jack Jr. also adds that the fairy tales, myths, and opera libretti that his father loved were very often about transformations.

Jack took roughly three different approaches to writing about transformation as a form of self-acceptance. One approach was to have characters go through unwanted transformation primarily for the comedic value of it. There are many *King Aroo* storylines that fall into this category, as do *Clotilda, The Fat Cat, Supermarket Magic,* and *Cindy Lou and the Witch's Dog*.

Round Robin (Prentice Hall, 1982) was Jack's latest book to fit into this category. True to his name, Round Robin loves eating so much that he becomes so large that he isn't able to fly south with his fellow robins. So he walks instead, and in the process he loses all of his extra weight. But once he reaches his destination, he immediately returns to his first love of eating and becomes large again. Though its message could be easily misinterpreted, at its heart *Round Robin* is a comedy about the tendency of birds—and people—to make the same mistakes again and again.

Jack's second approach to writing about transformation involved stories in which an alteration actually leads to the main character recognizing their inherent value. For example, in *The Blah*, Billy is empowered by his temporary transformation, and in "The Lonely Tree," a tree is transformed for the better by the presence of a community around her.

But perhaps Jack's most effective and touching exploration of transformation as a path to self-acceptance is *The Christmas Piñata*, published by Parents' Magazine Press in 1975. Set in Mexico, the story concerns a pot that has cracked in the kiln and been set aside. The cracked pot looks on sadly as the other pots are decorated with "gay shapes and bright colors," taken to the market to be sold, or used to carry water from the well. The pot finally finds a purpose when young Maria Gomez realizes it would be perfect for a piñata. And so covered with newspaper and colorful tissue paper, it's transformed into the centerpiece of the Las Posadas celebration and feels "terribly important." In the end, its broken pieces end up in a heap with the pieces of a "good" pot—once beautiful and useful—that has worn out. They have the following exchange:

> "We began the same and we ended the same," said one pile of bits.
> "Everybody does," said the other.
> "And in between, we were each useful in our own way," said one.
> "Everybody is," said the other.

The Caterpillar and the Polliwog (Prentice Hall, 1982) also demonstrates this approach well. Building on one of his favorite running gags in *King Aroo*, the book is about a tadpole who watches with envy as a caterpillar goes through the stages of becoming a butterfly, not realizing that he himself is at the same time becoming a frog right before our eyes. When he does discover the transformation, he's initially disappointed that he didn't become a butterfly too. But after the butterfly compliments him, he reflects and comes to accept the truth of her words: "I *am*, you know, a *very* handsome frog."

Both books serve as self-pep talks, with Jack reminding himself that even if he hadn't turned out the way he thought he would, he still turned out okay and he still has value. In the process, he provided comfort to all the kids and parents who felt similarly discouraged. As the moral of *The Christmas Piñata* reads, "For there is contentment in knowing that whoever you are, you're somebody."

The third way Jack wrote about transformation and self-acceptance was to have his main character discover that transformation wasn't what they wanted at all and that they much prefer being themselves. That's exactly what happens in *Just Only John*, *The Wizard of Wallaby Wallow*, and *Dooly and the Snortsnoot*, and it's also the basic plot of *Knee-High Nina* (Doubleday, 1980) and *The Once-Upon-a-Time Dragon* (Harcourt Brace Jovanovich, 1982).

Knee-High Nina is about a girl who gets sick of being too small to do things for herself, so she wishes not only to be big but for her parents to become small. As a result, they are all able to see from each other's perspective, and Nina realizes "she wasn't through being little yet."

The Once-Upon-a-Time Dragon was actually one of Jack's first children's book ideas, but it took many years to land at a publisher. The story concerns a dragon named Sam who loves bedtime stories so much "he went to bed 87 times a day, so it was always time for another story." Like Drexel Dragon did in *King Aroo* before him, Sam becomes convinced that he's actually a man who has been put under a spell. So he decides that he'll do a thirty-day body-building course to "be the man you want to become." He wants to become Mr. Johnson, a rotund, mustachioed fellow who is the happiest man Sam knows. The body-building course works, and Sam becomes the spitting image of Mr. Johnson, even down to his brown hat and suit.

Having retained his ability to breathe fire, Sam joins the circus and becomes a star attraction. But this leads him to neglect his body building and revert back to his original form. He gets fired, because "there isn't any novelty in a dragon breathing fire," and returns to his old life. The only difference is that he now has a stronger friendship with Mr. Johnson, to whom he reveals "I'm much more comfortable just being myself."

Sam wasn't necessarily dissatisfied with his transformation; he just couldn't maintain it. Perhaps Jack was recalling his own search for what it meant to "be himself," specifically his "Texas Jack" days, and how difficult it is to be something you're not. Jack knew the healthier approach was to accept who you are and learn self-love, but that could be equally difficult. So he had to keep reminding himself over and over again through his stories.

Though Jack didn't like books that were written only to teach a lesson or moral, he clearly recognized that his stories carried important ideas. He said:

> What I'm trying to do can be compared to a public swimming pool, which has a deep end and a shallow end. Whatever the reader's abilities are can be served by that. The very smallest child is going to be read to. Whoever is stuck with the job of reading has to get a little fun out of it too. So I try, without getting out of the child's range, to put something there that the reader, the adult, can enjoy also.

The irony is that in writing from a place of insecurity about the depth of his books, Jack imbued them with that very depth. What's more, he did it without sacrificing humor or kid appeal. He did it just by being himself.

Chapter 14

Just Only Jack (1984–1985)

In the last years of his life, Jack strove to find balance. "If there's something I want to do," he said in a 1985 interview, "I don't get myself involved in work to the point where I can't do it." But that didn't mean he became less of a homebody. His idea of fun was spending time with June, gardening, reading, and, yes, working.

He ventured out less and less, but Jack had two regular destinations. One was Rosengren's Books. Camille Rosengren had taken over managing the store in 1979 and continued to build it into a local cultural landmark. Jack could still occasionally be counted on to hold a release party for a new book there, but more often he came in as a customer. June was a voracious reader too, and that meant the Kents' book collection pushed toward ten thousand volumes and their house doubled as a library. "We only buy books on the subjects in which we're interested, but we're interested in virtually everything," Jack once said. "Our walls are bookshelves from floor to ceiling, making wallpaper unnecessary and picture-hanging nigh impossible."

A love of reading was a central part of Jack's identity, and he saw his books as a perfect way to spread that love to young people. He viewed his books as a sort of gateway drug. "Humor is my medium, but my purpose is serious," he said in a 1981 interview. "If a book of mine is fun, perhaps it will encourage the young reader to try another book sometime." In a different interview he put it this way: "I like to think that my little soufflés might instill an appetite for books in the wee folk and encourage them to sample weightier fare. Maybe they will learn to love books as I do."

King Aroo, March 6, 1956. Courtesy of Jack Kent Jr.

The only other place where Jack could be regularly found was at weekly services at St. Mark's Episcopal Church, though he rarely stuck around for coffee and fellowship. Located in downtown San Antonio, across from Travis Park, the church had a long history, including hosting the 1934 wedding of Lyndon and Lady Bird Johnson.

Jack and June's association with St. Mark's actually began in the late 1950s. The church also had a primary school and offered before and after childcare, a fact they advertised in a conscious outreach to single and working mothers. When Jack Jr. was ready to start school, Jack and June were still working at Ferguson Map Company, which wasn't far from St. Mark's. They enrolled Jack in the school, and eventually he was "nudged" to ask his parents why they didn't attend services. So, out of guilt they began going to church, but they found it to be a comfortable place for both of them. Jack even served on the vestry for a while, which Jack Jr. guesses "must have felt close to martyrdom for him" given his introverted nature.

Jack's journey to becoming a faithful churchgoer was not a straightforward one. His parents identified as Christian Scientists, but it's not known how closely they adhered to it. For most of his teen and early adult life, Jack seems to have kept religion at arm's length, treating it with the same intellectual curiosity that he treated everything else with. Among the scores of allusions Jack included in *King Aroo*, the Bible shows up only three times. The only hint of his parents' religion in the comic strip is in the way its characters are not bound by the laws of the material world (e.g., the weatherman controlling the weather or a dodo bird being ignorant of the fact that it's extinct), but this is played for laughs.

King Aroo, July 25, 1960. Courtesy of Jack Kent Jr.

And though science and religion aren't mutually exclusive, Jack's strong belief in science may have superseded any metaphysical beliefs. He often had his *King Aroo* characters challenge and misunderstand scientific principles, such as the dinosaur that wakes from hibernation and can't keep his balance because the world is no longer flat or the Hebefrenian judges who decide to revoke the law of gravity. Like most depictions of absurdity, this had the effect of celebrating and affirming the accumulated knowledge of experts.

When Jack Jr. was young, Jack made a point of teaching his son the lyrics to "It Ain't Necessarily So," a George and Ira Gershwin tune from *Porgy and Bess*. The song is a semihumorous list of doubts about the stories and teachings of the Bible and serves as a warning not to blindly believe everything you're told, as well as a justification for getting into a bit of trouble now and then.

Jack's children's books had no hint of religious dogma; they were much more likely to promote the value of empathy and kindness (as in "The Butterfly"), to espouse the power of ideas (as in *Mr. Meebles*), or to express the benefits of appreciating the world around you (as in *Clotilda*). "To me the world is a fascinating place," Jack said in a 1981 interview, "and my books are attempts at sharing feelings of wonder and pleasure."

This may explain what kept Jack returning to St. Mark's. The church claims its "core vocation" as being "to feed the hungry with real food, feed those who are hungry for knowledge and meaning, and feed those who are hungry for beauty and creativity."

. . .

Jack's retreat from the larger world was another transformation, but unlike his earlier shifts, it wasn't born of necessity. It was partially a reversion to his authentic self. We don't always think of introverts as capable of being charming, warm, and witty, but they can be, and Jack certainly was. He wasn't awkward, unfriendly, or shy, just someone who felt most comfortable with solitary pursuits and a small circle of people around him. The poet, author, and teacher Naomi Shihab Nye—who lived around the corner from the Kents—said June and Jack were content in each other's orbit. "There was a feeling of closeness, harmony, and solidarity between them that made it so they did not need a lot of outward stimulation to be happy."

Naomi and her husband Michael had moved into the King William neighborhood in 1979, but their connection with the Kents went back further than that. In 1967, when Naomi was a teenager, her family fled the coming war in Jerusalem, where they'd lived for just a year after relocating from St. Louis. They settled in San Antonio. Her father was a newspaper reporter by trade but needed a job. He went to the San Antonio Express and News building, marched into the newsroom, and said, "My name is Aziz Shihab. I'm Palestinian-Arab. I've been the editor for the last year at the *Jerusalem Times*, and I would like to work at this newspaper. I'd be willing to do anything. I'll even sweep your floors."

June, who was at that time in her second stint at the *Express*, was there to witness it, and was a part of a group of *Express* employees who urged the paper to hire Shihab. They did, and he would write for the paper for the next eight years before departing for the *Dallas Morning News*.

Naomi didn't realize right away that she lived near June, nor did she realize that Jack was a fellow author. In the course of one of her regular visits to local elementary schools, a school librarian asked her where she lived and then replied, "Oh, I bet you know that children's book author who refuses to come to our school." Subsequent conversations Naomi had with other librarians revealed a pattern: they'd all requested that Jack visit their school, and he'd refused every one of them, even when offered money.

"So I developed this mythos about Jack Kent the hermit," Naomi says. She sought out Jack's books, buying some at the Twig Book Shop and checking out others at the library. She loved them and became determined to meet their reclusive author. Naomi and Michael kept chickens in their yard, and so she gathered up a dozen eggs and wrote a note introducing herself, which included her phone number. Jack called soon after and invited her over.

Over subsequent visits Naomi established a friendship with both Jack and June. "They were very gracious in that way that's so lovely and old world. June would make me tea or lemonade. They would bring things out to show me, and I always loved that. I would sit in this chair and feel really cozy like a child again. There was warmth in the circle with the three of us."

As for Jack, she discovered that he was not a curmudgeonly misanthrope. "He seemed like a humorist to me," she says. "A cheerful, laid back, relaxed, oh-don't-worry-about-it kind of guy." Eventually Naomi felt comfortable enough to challenge Jack on his policy of not speaking at schools. "I don't make speeches," he told her. "If you speak to a group, how could you possibly know what you could say that would be appropriate for all of those ears to hear at once?"

This was an excuse Jack had devised, and a somewhat flimsy one at that. No person who writes books for a living feels they don't have something to share with a wide audience. Part of Jack's reluctance to put himself in front of a crowd may have been a fear of public speaking and another manifestation of his insecurity.

But Naomi's prodding did result in one notable success. Naomi was a member of the Texas Institute of Letters, an authors' organization that gives annual awards for the best work by Texas writers. Assigned to judge the children's category one year, Naomi and her fellow judges were utterly dismayed by the poor quality of the entrants and struggled to pick winners they felt were actually worthy. Naomi went to Jack afterward and told him he needed to enter the next year, because his books were so much better than the competition.

So Jack reluctantly submitted *The Once-Upon-a-Time Dragon* and was shocked when he received the notification that he'd won the award for best book for young people, along with a four hundred dollar prize. The award was to be given at a ceremony in April 1983, but Jack would not commit to attend, especially because his notification letter requested he give a short acceptance speech.

Disappointed, Naomi grudgingly agreed to accept on his behalf. Then, to her astonishment, Jack showed up at the ceremony, *and* he got up and gave a speech. He talked about how *The Once-Upon-a-Time Dragon* had been rejected fifty-two times before finding a publisher. He said editors told him over and over again that the book was for adults, not children. But he kept sending it out because he was confident that kids would be smart enough to get it.

Jack just 8 months before his death, 1985. Courtesy of *San Antonio Express-News*/ZUMA Press.

124   Just Only Jack (1984–1985)

"He was phenomenal," Naomi recalls. "He was the best recipient of the evening." Afterward, the accomplished author John Graves came up to Naomi and said, "That guy from San Antonio was a charmer. What an uplift!" Later Jack admitted to her that he'd enjoyed himself greatly, and Naomi pointed out that he'd been depriving himself of all the fun he could have had talking to groups of kids. He didn't change his policy on visiting schools, but the next year, he submitted *Silly Goose* to the Texas Institute of Letters, and he won again.

• • •

In June 1984 Peg Kent passed away, just a couple months shy of her eighty-sixth birthday. Though it was very tough on Jack, it was also a relief. In her final years Peg suffered from dementia, and Jack and June cared for her themselves, which was a daily challenge.

This is partly why Jack's writing pace slowed a bit during this time. He released a total of seven books in 1984 and 1985, three of his own and four for other authors. In the latter category was Charles Keller's *Grime Doesn't Pay: Law and Order Jokes* (Prentice Hall, 1984), Howard Goldsmith's *The Twiddle Twins' Haunted House* (Caedmon, 1985), *Q Is for Duck,* and *Easy as Pie* (both from Houghton Mifflin, 1985). The latter two books, both by Michael Folsom, are full of little visual flights of imagination that were such a Jack Kent trademark, such as a loon depicted dressed as Napoleon, complete with his wing tucked into the front of his shirt.

Jack's self-authored books from this time period found him trying some new tricks through familiar lenses. *Jim Jimmy James*—Jack's third and final book for Susan Hirschman's Greenwillow—is a book that's simultaneously simple and complex. On the surface it seems to be a straightforward tale of a boy using the mirror to keep himself entertained, a sort of echo of the Marx Brothers' mirror routine in *Duck Soup*. But a closer look uncovers a more complex theme about the dangers of becoming too self-involved.

When Jack's story begins, Jim Jimmy James is stuck inside on a rainy day. Out of boredom, he begins interacting with himself in the mirror on his closet door. He performs so many actions that his reflection gets tired and falls out of the mirror. The reflection introduces himself as James Jimmy Jim, and the pair begin to play together. But the problem is that James can't do anything that Jim doesn't do first, and that proves to be no fun. In the end of *Jim Jimmy James*, James Jimmy Jim returns to the mirror and invites Jim to come inside. Jim refuses. Instead, he looks out the window, sees the rain has stopped, and goes out to play.

In Jack's original manuscribble, the story was one page longer and ended with a wry joke. The page followed Jim outside, where he sees James reflected in a puddle. "I'm glad you could come out and play, too!" he says. Hirschman asked Jack to remove that page, and with that seemingly small request, completely changed the tone and theme of the story.

Jack had written many stories featuring a character that is somehow unhappy or bored with themselves. He did it again here, but Jim's discontent is resolved not by becoming someone else and then realizing how much better it is to be one's own self but by self-reflecting until it becomes tedious. Only in looking beyond the self can one truly appreciate the world.

Joey (Prentice Hall, 1984) is about a kangaroo whose mother worries about him ("as mothers do") being out in the world, so she puts him in her pouch and encourages his friends to come visit. This results in a crowded party in the pouch in which the kids watch TV and listen to records. Mother reaches her breaking point when the kids form their own rock band and throws them all out, including Joey. The conclusion reveals a truth about parenthood: it's difficult to let your children go, but it's equally difficult to keep them close.

Though there was great love between Jack and Jack Jr., they'd had their share of clashes. Jack had addressed the friction between parenthood and childhood before (as in *The Grown-Up Day*, *The Blah*, *Knee-High Nina*, and "The Runaway"), but this was the first time he'd taken the parent's perspective.

Joey depicts the mother kangaroo's pouch as comically large, a pocket dimension akin to Snoopy's doghouse, just as he had done with Mr. Pennipost's pouch in *King Aroo*. Ideas from Jack's *King Aroo* days had continually shown up as elements in his children's books, showing that even though Jack's career had a very clear demarcation between newspaper cartoonist and children's author, the two were inextricable. *King Aroo* had informed both *Little Peep* and *The Biggest Shadow in the Zoo*, both published in 1981. The former book is a clear echo of a May 1951 *King Aroo* sequence in which Harold Rooster teaches his nephew Tommy the ropes (Jack uses the same sound—"peep-a-deedle-peep"—for the young rooster's attempts). The latter is an expansion of a January 1954 *King Aroo* in which Mr. Elephant panics because he thinks his shadow has fallen over a cliff. In 1985 Jack placed an original story in a second grade school reader that could have just as easily been a *King Aroo* Sunday strip. Titled "An Old Kitten Is a Cat," the piece is an illustration of the classic Telephone game, in which a message is passed from person to person, changing in form and content along the way. Jack's version starts with Jenny telling her friend she got a new kitten and ends with Carmen believing that a robber stole Jenny's purse (with her kitten inside).

• • •

Where *Joey* and *Jim Jimmy James* explored new(ish) territory, Jack's final book—*Joey Runs Away* (Prentice Hall, 1985)—was a return to one of his most enduring themes. This sequel to *Joey* finds the young kangaroo and his mother once again at odds, this time over the fact that he won't clean his room (which, again, is located in her pouch). Tired of being nagged, and overwhelmed by the task before him, Joey decides to leave home. This leads to a comical sequence in which other potential tenants—including a bear, a giraffe, and many rabbits—tour the vacant room. Joey, meanwhile, tries out other places to live, including a pelican's beak and a mail bag. He quickly becomes homesick and realizes how much he liked his mother's pouch.

Like its predecessor, *Joey Runs Away* is a funny look at the parent-child dynamic. Unlike the first book, this one deals with the child's perspective and gives us this exchange:

"Joey, come clean up your room!" Mother kangaroo said. "I've told you a hundred times!"

"Eight times," Joey mumbled. He had kept count.

This was a clear echo of 1971's "The Runaway," in which the title character says, "There's a limit to how much 'DO THIS!' and 'DON'T

DO THAT!' a boy can take!" That character also leaves home out of frustration, only to realize how good he had it, and this was an idea Jack kept returning to.

In *King Aroo*, Jack more than once had characters run away from home, only to admit they didn't actually know where their home was. *Fly Away Home* (1969) was all about trying to find the right home, with the girl trying out all sorts of unsuitable places before reaching the right one. In the 1970 story "The Lovely Day," a weather forecaster tires of "fair and mild" weather and goes off to find other kinds, only to realize how much he liked "fair and mild." In 1979's *Piggy Bank Gonzales*, a piggy bank runs away and falls in with a group of real pigs that take advantage of him, and this leads him to realize just how loved he was at his home.

These stories were all variations on Jack's theme of transformation and self-acceptance, but with the transformation being geographical instead of physical. The fact that "Joey Runs Away" and "The Runaway" involve parents and children is telling, because these stories can be seen as expressions of Jack's feelings about his itinerant childhood. He seems to acknowledge that by staying constantly on the move, Ralph and Peg had denied him the comfort, calm, and sense of security that having a permanent home can bring. And yet he was also likely empathetic to his parents' susceptibility to new starts. He had been there himself, as in his and June's unsuccessful effort to permanently relocate to Cuernavaca.

These stories are also about where Jack was at this point in his life. In *Piggy Bank Gonzales*, the piggy bank learns to appreciate a home that's "quiet and comfortable and not very exciting." After spending so much of his life on the move both emotionally and physically, and after enduring multiple failed attempts, Jack had achieved his happily ever after. He lived in the home he'd designed, surrounded by books, occupied with work he enjoyed, living with his true love, and immersed in nature. In 1983, he wrote:

> The San Antonio River as it flows past us is a modest stream, having been born of springs just north of the city. What with the river and the trees, it's as if we lived in the country. Our neighbors are squirrels and raccoons and opossums and fish and

turtles and frogs and a wide variety of birds. With a wife like June to share it, surely Heaven must be something like this.

The cruel thing is, Jack didn't get long to enjoy it. Sometime in the early 1980s, routine bloodwork revealed that Jack had polycythemia vera (PV), a rare cancer that causes blood to thicken and flow at a slower pace than normal. PV increases the risk of blood clots, heart attack, and stroke and can lead to even more serious blood diseases. Jack kept the bad news from June and Jack Jr. and didn't pursue treatment.

In late 1984, Jack learned that his PV had progressed to acute myelogenous leukemia (AML). The prognosis was grim. One of the main complications of the AML was that Jack's blood would no longer clot, so any injury that bled was potentially life-threatening. He had to get an electric razor, which he hated because it felt like an extravagance. He needed an implant for a chemotherapy pump, but the places where they tried to implant it wouldn't heal. His sister Mary Lou and Jack Jr. made weekly donations of platelets, in the hopes they'd be a transfusion match.

Much of Jack's last eleven months were spent in and out of doctors' offices, and it was a difficult and dispiriting time. But he continued to work. Just six weeks before his death, Jack was still making submissions to the likes of *Cricket Magazine*. He had two books in the works that he ran out of time to finish—*The Gorfu*, to be published by Harcourt in 1986, and illustrations for Joe Hayes's *No Way José* (the book was instead published with pictures by New Mexico resident Lucy Jelinck).

On Jack's final day, 18 October 1985, he had gone to the hospital and his doctor discovered he'd started to bleed in his brain. It was inoperable. The doctor called a family meeting and said, "Jack, you asked me to tell you, and so I'm telling you. It's time to die."

Jack replied, "Thank you."

Following a progressive paralysis, Jack fell into unconsciousness and died that night. "It was a gentle end to an awful summer and fall," Jack Jr. says. And it was an all too early end to a fantastically creative life.

• • •

Jack was laid to rest in a simple graveside service presided over by the rector of St. Mark's Episcopal. Mary Lou, Dudley, and their children's families attended, as did June's best friend Annabeth Mays and her husband Bob. Camille and Frank Rosengren paid their respects, along with a smattering of writers and newspaper staffers.

After Jack's death Naomi Shihab Nye wrote a poem about Jack called "Rain Falling into the River—That Moment When They Merge." It was published in her book *Mint* in 1991.

In a cottage by a river a man made stories. He lived so fully in his room it was hard to get him out. His room grew jungles, revising itself with light. I think he would stand in his room staring out at rain falling into the river and wonder why people went anywhere to begin with—this world of avenues fashioning, tugging, offering what we learn to need—he could see the sadness in that without even entering it. Whole catalogues of sadnesses—species, radiant wings, and eyes. He chose his quiet kind and planted banana leaf palms. He drew little men who turn into donkeys. Little girls who fly into flowers and sleep there. When people invited him to come and talk to them about being an artist, he declined. It was hard to talk to more than one person at a time, to say the right words to enter so many ears at once. Better the river's quiet pulse, the heaping mountains of cloud gathering silently on any horizon, tilting the day a different way. He drew a little boy and girl who wanted to be grown-up until bedtime came—then they were ready to be small again. Sometimes when I can't sleep I think of his pen in the room next to the river, shaping, shaping, a jeweled crown, a kangaroo, a billowing tree. Since he died he's rewritten the whole neighborhood.

Epilogue

Ever After (1986 and Beyond)

One of Jack's dying wishes had been that his manuscripts and artwork go to the Kerlan Collection, a children's literature archive housed at the University of Minnesota. The collection's curator at the time, Karen Nelson Hoyle, had visited Jack and June a few years earlier to tell them about the Kerlan, which would preserve the work and provide access to it for scholars. So in the summer of 1987, June and Jack Jr. loaded up their station wagon and drove to Minneapolis.

Along the way they stopped in Askov, Minnesota, where June had a marvelous time attending her fiftieth high school reunion. Her connections to the area were still strong. She'd maintained an epistolary friendship with Arol Hansen, a high school friend, and kept up a subscription to the *Askov American*. In Minneapolis, they had lunch with Dr. Hoyle and then deposited Jack's work.

Among the materials June and Jack Jr. took to the Kerlan were unpublished projects in various states of completion. There were sketched-out pages for a 1977 nonfiction book *All about Bones*, to be done under the jokey pseudonym S. Tibia Clavicle. Jack had some good ideas for the book, but the technical demands of the subject were not a great match for his cartoony style. There were also two pages each of preliminary sketches for new editions of *Alice in Wonderland* and *Pinocchio*, both done in 1973. A seemingly abandoned 1971 project called *Jack Kent's Book of Words* was a clear precursor to *Jack Kent's Hop, Skip and Jump Book*, though unlike that book's two-page spreads, the earlier one featured a series of numbered sequences that gave Jack the chance to present various nouns and verbs.

Epilogue: Ever After (1986 and Beyond) 131

A page from the unpublished *Jack Kent's Book of Words*, date unknown. Jack Kent Papers. Kerlan Collection, Children's Literature Research Collections, University of Minnesota Libraries, Minneapolis. Courtesy of Jack Kent Jr. and the Kerlan Collection.

Jack had a small handful of posthumous releases. Sometime before his death, he had submitted to Random House a story about a boy and girl who take a trip to town to buy ice cream only to become distracted multiple times on the way home. The publisher gave it to author Gail Herman to adapt, and she converted it into an easy reader with only forty-seven different words. The book was published as *Ice Cream Dream* in 1990, with illustrations by R. W. Alley.

Jack's submissions to *Cricket Magazine* also ended up seeing print, though much later than he could have ever imagined. Thirteen years after his father's death, Jack Jr. was surprised to receive a check for publication of the illustrated poem "The Early Bird." A return to a recurring *King Aroo* joke, "The Early Bird" tells the story of a wren who gets up "at the crack of dawn" only to find the worm had stayed home "with a rather sore throat and a cold in the head." So the wren has to eat noodles that look like worms instead. The poem showed up in a 1998 issue of the younger readers' version of *Cricket*, *Ladybug*. It was accompanied by a one-page bio of Jack written by Jack Jr.

And then, another seven years later, *Cricket* accepted another of Jack's poems, "The Firefly." It starts off like an ode to finding wonder in nature, with a narrator questioning how the insect is able to light up. The firefly's reply offers a Kentian twist: "Bioluminescence is the oxidation of an enzyme/or protoplast called luciferin or luciferase." Jack likely included an illustration with the poem, but in the magazine it's accompanied by a piece by artist Susan Estelle Kwas.

• • •

For a few years Jack's children's book work lived on with young readers through libraries, teachers, book club selections, and video adaptations. Children's entertainer Bob Keeshan read *There's No Such Thing as a Dragon* on an early 1980s episode of his show *Captain Kangaroo*. *The Wizard of Wallaby Wallow* was adapted as a short animated film (retitled *The Wizard*) by Weston Woods in 1985. In 1988 the same company made films of *Joey Runs Away* and *The Caterpillar and the Polliwog*. The following year, Golden Books put out a VHS containing animated versions of *Merry Mother Goose*, *Mrs. Mooley*, and *There's No Such Thing as a Dragon*. All of these short films were shown on children's programs and in schools. In addition, Jack's books—among them *Socks for Supper*, *The Caterpillar and the Polliwog*, *The Wizard of Wallaby Wallow*—were a regular feature in school readers from a variety of educational publishers in the late 1980s.

Kent Cummins, who became a juggler, magician, and performer by trade, kept his uncle's work alive with a traveling presentation for schools and libraries called "A Tribute to Jack Kent." Kent would read a few of his favorite Jack Kent books and tell stories about them. For example, after sharing 1981's *The Scribble Monster*, Kent would recall

Epilogue: Ever After (1986 and Beyond)   133

childhood memories playing "the scribble game": "Uncle Jack would draw a scribble and I would try to turn it into something. I would then draw a scribble and Uncle Jack would turn it into a face or an animal or a fire-breathing dragon, or a castle, complete with princess!"

Besides serving as one of Kent's creative inspirations, Jack also used his talents to support his nephew's endeavors. In the late 1970s Kent started a chain of delis in Austin, Texas called The SamWitch Shops. Jack drew five variations of a hook-nosed witch brandishing a wand to serve as the restaurant's mascot (the witch was a dead ringer for the one in *Cindy Lou and the Witch's Dog* and Jack's 1979 scratch-and-sniff book *Supermarket Magic*). Jack also designed the logo—a juggling rabbit emerging from a hat—for Kent's magic act, the Fantastic Kent Cummins. A version of the logo still stands today as the logo of the long-running summer program Kent started in 1993, Fantastic Magic Camp. Jack never asked for payment for doing this or the SamWitch illustrations. "Not that I ever offered," Kent laughs.

• • •

As the 1980s became the 1990s, Jack's books began to steadily drop out of print. Parents' Magazine Press shuttered in the mideighties after its parent company was bought by the *Saturday Evening Post*, relegating eleven of Jack's books to publishing purgatory. In 1989, *Little Peep* and *Round Robin* were both reissued, giving them rare second life, but soon only stalwarts such as *The Fat Cat*, *There's No Such Thing as a Dragon*, and *I Was Walking Down the Road* would be left. Jack never worked with an agent, leaving June to manage his literary estate. This made it more difficult for his books to live on past their natural span.

Of course they lived on in an immeasurable way in the millions of young readers who experienced them at a crucial moment in their lives. And because of this Jack's books have a way of showing up in surprising places. Before he became a controversial author, University of Toronto psychology professor Jordan B. Peterson was most known for a 2002 lecture called "Slaying the Dragon within Us" in which he used *There's No Such Thing as a Dragon* as a way to discuss fear of the unknown and of confronting the problems that are in front of our faces.

In 2017, NPR produced a podcast called *S-Town*, concerning an eccentric man named John B. McLemore. In the third episode, "Tedious and Brief," McLemore's friend Tyler Goodson talked about the book he read aloud at John's funeral:

Brian Reed: What's the name of the book that you brought to his funeral?

Tyler: *Just Only John.* I got it in there. I read it to the girls last night. And it was everything I could do to finish it. And I gave the girls a hug and tried to get out [of] the room as fast as I could, because I [was] just fucking crying my eyes out over that damn book. But it's just a kid['s] book, and it's [about] a kid, he wanted to be a fucking dog or a tiger or something like that. And some witch put a spell on him, and if [he] said he was this, he would be that. But he wouldn't know how to act being that. So everything he wanted to be, he's just John.

In 2010, artist, writer, and editor Shaenon Garrity wrote a piece about *Cindy Lou and the Witch's Dog* for *The Comics Journal*. She called it "the first comic book I ever read" and said the illustration in which Prince trees over fifty cats is "one of my favorite single panels in any comic ever." She lauded Jack's loose line work, his cute but funny character designs, and his organic coloring, concluding that because of *Cindy Lou and the Witch's Dog* being such a formative reading experience for her, she has been spoiled: "Again and again, comic books disappoint me by not being drawn by Jack Kent."

Jack's legacy in comic strips is one of quiet influence, and it's not difficult to find other strips that mined the same veins of humor that Jack had opened up. Johnny Hart and Brent Parker's *The Wizard of Id* debuted just a few months before *King Aroo* took its final bow. The concept of the strip will sound very familiar: it followed a king who lived in a castle surrounded by a moat and who ruled over a kingdom of daffy subjects. He even had a retinue who dabbled in magic. Unlike *King Aroo*, however, the strip was a massive hit. In addition to running in thousands of newspapers, it won multiple awards from the National Cartoonist's Society. In 1972, Bob Thaves's *Frank and Earnest*

Epilogue: Ever After (1986 and Beyond)　　　　135

King Aroo, 1 Mar. 1961. Courtesy of Jack Kent Jr.

debuted. Built on *King Aroo*-like puns and wordplay, the strip was also a huge success and won its creator many awards.

If Jack felt any bitterness about his exit from the world of daily cartooning, it didn't show. He continued to subscribe to all three San Antonio papers and faithfully read the comics page for each one. Of course he was a fan of *Frank and Earnest*. Jack Jr. says he wishes his father had lived to see Bill Watterson's *Calvin and Hobbes*: "I can think of few cartoonists who shared Daddy's insight into the strange mixture of innocence, jaded awareness of more than we'd like to think, whimsy, and savagery that goes in the mind of a child."

A 1 March 1961 *King Aroo* featured the king prominently displaying his Christmas tree, depicted as a scraggly twig adorned with a single bulb. One immediately thinks of the undernourished tree Charlie Brown buys in the 1965 animated special *A Charlie Brown Christmas*, even down to the crisscrossed wooden planks at the bottom. One of the special's cocreators, Lee Mendelson, credited Hans Christian Andersen's "The Fir Tree" as an inspiration, but Charles Schulz *was* a *King Aroo* fan (and in turn, Jack loved *Peanuts*).

Other cartoonists were more direct in their tributes to Jack and *King Aroo*. In the mid-1960s, before *King Aroo* was even finished, Belgian cartoonist Marc Sleen's *Nero* featured a King Aroo lookalike as the monarch of a fictional kingdom called Slobobavia. And in a series of three *Li'l Abner* Sunday strips in 1969, Al Capp told a fairy tale about a creature called the "kingaroo." King Stubbornovsky takes the kingaroo in when it's young, not knowing that when kingaroos become fully grown they eat kings. A September 2010 edition of Bill Griffith's absurd and surreal *Zippy* found characters sharing nominations for the yearly "Irving Award" for best daily comic strip of the past. The character Jet Pinkston says, "I'd say 'King Aroo' by Jack Kent because he uses big words."

And in a very real way, Jack's work helped bring other cartoonists' work to prominence. Stanleigh Arnold's formation of Golden Gate Features to distribute *King Aroo* would turn out to be a precursor to Arnold's very successful career as manager of Chronicle Features Syndicate. There he helped launch the careers of Garry Trudeau (*Doonesbury*) and Gary Larson (*The Far Side*), among many others.

There are also elements of children's literature that *King Aroo* seems to have either predicted or influenced. A June 1953 strip finds Yupyop's imagination coming to life in the form of a horned, round-eyed monster with sharp teeth. "And you'd better watch out," it warns, "'Cause Yupyop's imagination is wild!" It's hard not to think of the creatures Max encounters in Maurice Sendak's *Where the Wild Things Are*, which would be published ten years later (and which Jack would seemingly draw inspiration from for *The Blah*).

A late 1953 storyline finds King Aroo going through the grandfather clock into the "dark recesses of time." Here he meets a watch dog, a dog with a clock for a body. This will be very familiar to fans of Norton Juster and Jules Feiffer's 1961 classic *The Phantom Tollbooth*, a book that shares *King Aroo*'s love for absurd personification and wordplay. And a September 1960 storyline concerns a very hungry goat named Gregory, bringing to mind Mitchell Sharmat and José Aruego's 1980 book *Gregory, the Terrible Eater*, which also features a goat, though the joke there is that this Gregory will only eat "normal" food.

And finally *King Aroo* seems to have direct successors in the realm of television. Since it was developed while *King Aroo* was still running, it's difficult to say whether or not Jay Ward and Bill Scott took inspiration from Jack's work for *The Rocky and Bullwinkle Show* (1959–1964), but the similarities are striking. As Bruce Canwell points out, "They both have different levels of appeal for a variety of age groups, and both succeed in never talking down to anyone in the audience." A love of puns and absurdity ran through both, as did the skewering of fairy tales (the satirical "Fractured Fairy Tales" segments in *Rocky and*

Epilogue: Ever After (1986 and Beyond)   137

Bullwinkle). A moose in a 16 November 1952 strip even looks similar to Bullwinkle. Jack, for his part, was a fan of the show.

Jack also loved irreverent and absurd comedies that could have just as well come from his own mind: *Monty Python's Flying Circus, That Was the Week That Was, Rowan and Martin's Laugh-In,* and *The Muppet Show.* The latter especially bears many of the hallmarks of Jack's work on *King Aroo.* Both the strip and the show delighted in scenarios in which—as author Christopher Finch wrote in the 1981 making-of book *Of Muppets and Men*—"everything is taken to its illogical conclusion."

None of this is to level an accusation that the creative people behind these comics, books, and programs stole from Jack. It's very possible they never saw *King Aroo* before or after their own acts of creation. But it is to say that Jack's ideas and sensibilities and approach were adopted and amplified by others, with much more success than Jack ever had.

· · ·

King Aroo spent many years spoken of in fond and reverent tones by those who remembered it firsthand or were able to track down a copy of the 1953 collection. Richard Marschall's entry on the strip in 1976's *The World Encyclopedia of Comics* stated, "*King Aroo* certainly belongs in the uncrowned class of such creations as *Little Nemo, Krazy Kat, Barnaby,* and *Pogo*; an 'intellectual' strip not aimed at any particular age or readership group, but cherished by cults in various categories." Bill Blackbeard and Martin Williams's 1977 *The Smithsonian Collection of Newspaper Comics* described *King Aroo* as "one of the most celebrated strips of the recent past in the comics, but celebrated largely among devotees of comics." (Jack himself picked the strips that accompanied the volume, a sequence from 26–31 Mar. 1956.) Writing about Jack in a 1981 *Something about the Author,* Denis Wepman stated that *King Aroo* "was much quoted for its verbal wit and loved for its narrative absurdity and visual charm."

For comics fans, *King Aroo* made sporadic and tantalizing appearances. The August 1986 issue of *Nemo: The Classic Comics Library* featured *King Aroo* on its cover and published over five months' worth of daily strips (Mar.–Aug. 1953), along with a brief introduction by Richard Marschall. He wrote of Jack's artwork, "His brushline was casual in the extreme, but its economy only masked the flawless composition and spotting of both props and white spaces in his work." In his 1996 encyclopedia 100 *Years of American Comics*, comics expert Maurice Horn described *King Aroo* as "an engaging blend of twisted fairy-tale nonsense story, fantasy yarn, and mock epic" and marveled that Jack's "imagination never flagged."

It wasn't until 2002, when comics editor and historian Tom Devlin wrote an article about Jack for a special edition of *The Comics Journal*, that *King Aroo* began to rise again in the public consciousness. "All Hail Jack Kent" featured a career overview, twelve Sunday *King Aroo* strips in color, and Devlin's loving assessment of the strip itself. "Every time I read the strip," he wrote, "I picture Kent at his drawing board, giggling away."

In 2005 comics writer Mark Evanier wrote on his blog that he believed James Childress's 1970s strip *Conchy* deserved a reprint collection. He said in response to that blog entry he received a phone call from his frequent collaborator Sergio Aragonés (and Jack's fan-tuned *Mad Magazine* colleague), who said that he agreed about *Conchy* but felt *King Aroo* was a higher priority. Evanier wrote that *King Aroo* was hard to describe. "You kind of have to see it . . . and I hope that someday soon, we'll all be able to."

In early 2010 he got that wish when the Library of American Comics (LoAC), an imprint of publisher IDW, put out a collection of the first two years of *King Aroo* strips using the original proofs from McClure Syndicate. Sergio Aragonés wrote an introduction for the volume, and LoAC's cofounder, Bruce Canwell, researched and wrote a biography of Jack. The latter represented the first in-depth examination of Jack's life. Unsurprisingly, given Canwell's job and background, he focused greatly on Jack's correspondence with cartoonists. The piece also included a generous amount of rare artwork from all phases of Jack's career.

Nearly simultaneously with the publication of the book, Burgin Streetman—who had written about Jack many times on her blog about vintage children's books—wrote an article about Jack for the *San Antonio Current*, the city's free alternative weekly paper. Her piece illuminated his personality and his work in children's books and made a plea for Jack's work to live on. "His books are still out there, just waiting to be loved again," she wrote. "It would be a damn shame to see them disappear forever." The next month, Naomi Shihab Nye held an event at Pearl Brewery sharing her memories of Jack.

Two years later LoAC published the second volume of *King Aroo*, containing strips from 1952 to 1954, and the conclusion of Canwell's biography of Jack. Canwell now counts the *King Aroo* reprint volumes among his proudest achievements. The *King Aroo* renaissance didn't last—there was no third volume—but it brought the strip back into the light and helped to cement it in the firmament of comic strip history.

• • •

June Kent, unfortunately, didn't live to see Jack's work brought back into the spotlight.

After Jack's death, June continued to live much as she had before: remaining close to home, reading voraciously, and visiting with her friend Annabeth. The only major change was the emergence of a love of watching basketball, especially the hometown NBA team, the Spurs. This didn't come out of nowhere. Her brother Howard had been captain of the Askov High School basketball team, and June claimed to have tried out for the University of Minnesota women's basketball team but lost her chance when she "knocked out" the coach with an errant pass. Speaking of Howard, June continued to visit him monthly.

Naomi Nye often observed June taking a daily walk to the post office located at South Main and Durango. She wore a trench coat, neatly belted, and walked with a regal stride, carrying a sack of mail back and forth (most likely correspondence with Jack's various publishers). If Naomi was out in her garden she and June would chat, sometimes trading neighborhood gossip.

When Naomi's son, Madison, turned two, June brought over paper grocery bags filled with fifty of Jack's books and a note that said, "I hope you will enjoy these as you get older." Madison treasured those books, and now Michael and Naomi read them to their grandson. She says, "Jack's books are more fun to read than other books for

Final panel from a valentine Jack made for June in 1977. Courtesy of Jack Kent Jr.

kids because they are so smart and sophisticated." She points to her favorite of Jack's books as an example. "In *Clotilda* where it says, 'She sat down on a daisy to feel sorry for herself in comfort.' In comfort! There's a subtlety there that might miss children but an adult reading that to a child is going to identify with that very much."

On one occasion after Naomi's poem about Jack had been published, June surprised her by appearing in the Nyes' driveway and declaring, "You got it wrong, if that piece is about Jack. That is NOT what made him tick, or write. It is NOT as you described." Naomi, who had been in the middle of trimming the vines on her front fence, was too thunderstruck to properly respond. She says she ended up feeling "presumptuous and foolish" for not consulting with June before publishing the poem. However, Jack Jr.—who did not read the poem until 2020—found it to be an insightful and accurate portrait of his father in his final years, perhaps a bit "too accurate" for his mother's comfort.

In the mid-1990s, June was diagnosed with high blood pressure, but she didn't make any lifestyle changes or seek out treatment. Jack Jr. believes as a result she had a series of transient ischemic attacks,

Epilogue: Ever After (1986 and Beyond)   141

or ministrokes. By 1999 she'd begun to show signs of dementia, and ultimately she died in hospice in February 2000.

June had been a pilot and a reporter and a mother and an organizer, but for all of her and Jack's individual accomplishments in life, they'd consider finding one another to be their greatest. Just a couple of years before his death, Jack said, "The nicest thing that ever happened to me was when a local newspaper subscribed to my comic strip and sent a reporter to interview me. I married her and lived happily ever after."

• • •

Jack Jr. worked in Houston as an architect for many years, but when the Houston economy took a downturn in the mid-1980s, which coincided with his father's leukemia diagnosis, Jack decided to leave the firm and Houston. Jack and June had purchased some land in Wimberly, in the hill country sixty miles northeast of San Antonio, partially as an "escape hatch" during a time when the Kents' house was under the threat of condemnation due to its proximity to the flood-prone San Antonio River. Jack Jr. got permission from his parents to build a house on the land in Wimberly, with the plan that he'd live there and open his own architecture firm in nearby Blanco. When Jack Jr. told his parents of the plan, Jack said, "You're doing what I did," meaning that he was striking out on his own the way Jack had after the end of *King Aroo*.

Also like his father, Jack Jr. eventually made a midlife career change. By the early 1990s, the economic downturn had spread across Texas, so he gave up architecture and enrolled at the University of Texas–Austin, where he studied philosophy, ecology, evolution, systematics, and population biology. After earning his doctorate, he lectured at the university for a few years.

Following his mother's death, Jack Jr. relocated to San Antonio, moving into the family home on Johnson Street. He took a position in San Antonio as a staff scientist at the Texas Biomedical Research Institute.

He also found love, with the help of Naomi Shihab Nye. After seeing both Jack Jr. and her friend Susan Athene at a fundraiser for

142 Epilogue: Ever After (1986 and Beyond)

Keystone School, Naomi had a lightning strike of inspiration and decided to play matchmaker. She invited herself and Susan over to Jack Jr.'s house for drinks and then excused herself almost immediately. Within a month, Jack Jr. and Susan had decided to get married. "It was perfect," Naomi says. "They're both so kind, so gentle. They're just solid, through-and-through good people."

In 2019 Susan encouraged Jack Jr. to take his father's collection of signed comic strips to the *Antiques Roadshow*'s visit to the McNay Art Museum in San Antonio. He ended up meeting with appraiser Kathleen Guzman, who gushed over the rarity and quality of the collection, specifically Jack's *Krazy Kat* Sunday strip, an early *Prince Valiant*, and a *Mickey Mouse* Sunday "signed by Walt Disney" (really cartoonist Floyd Gottfredson). She astonished Jack Jr. by valuing the entire collection at somewhere between 105,000 to 140,000 dollars. The segment aired on PBS in early 2020, not long after Heritage Auctions sold Jack's collection in pieces, sending it off to be cherished by other collectors.

• • •

Jack Kent's ultimate legacy is the rich body of work he left behind: comic strips and children's books full of wit, whimsy, and wisdom, just waiting to be discovered. He made us laugh, and he made us reflect, and most of all he reminded us that life is a process of learning and relearning to be yourself, "because somebody has to, and you're the closest."

Acknowledgments

Much gratitude to Jack Kent Jr. for his generosity, insight, and counsel.

Great appreciation to those who aided me on this journey: Ann Arnold, Susan Athene, Sarah Barchas, Craig Bridgman, Kent Cummins, Burgin Streetman, Lauren Goss, Misty Harris, Susan Hirschman, Karen Nelson Hoyle, Katrina Kochneva, Denis Kitchen, Susan Liberator, Caitlyn Marineau, Rebecca Matalon, Naomi Shihab Nye, Cris Piquinela, Rebecca Russell, Ansen Seale, and Michael Tisserand.

Thanks to the manuscript's readers, Kelly Burch, and the team at University Press of Mississippi, especially Lisa McMurtray, Katie Keene, and Pete Halverson.

Much love to Wendy, Peter, and Theo, who continue to graciously tolerate my writing projects.

Appendix

I. JACK KENT'S PUBLISHED BOOKS FOR CHILDREN

As author and illustrator

Just Only John (1968, Parents' Magazine Press)
Fly Away Home (1969, David McKay Co.)
The Grown-Up Day (1969, Parents' Magazine Press)
Clotilda (1969, Random House)
Mr. Elephant's Birthday Party (1969, Houghton Mifflin)
The Blah (1970, Parents' Magazine Press)
The Fat Cat (1971, Parents' Magazine Press)
The Wizard of Wallaby Wallow (1971, Parents' Magazine Press)
Dooly and the Snortsnoot (1972, Putnam)
Jack Kent's Fables of Aesop (1972, Parents' Magazine Press)
Mrs. Mooley (1973, Golden Books)
Twelve Days of Christmas (1973, Parents' Magazine Press)
Jack Kent's Hop, Skip and Jump Book (1974, Random House)
More Fables of Aesop (1974, Parents' Magazine Press)
The Christmas Piñata (1975, Parents' Magazine Press)
There's No Such Thing as a Dragon (1975, Golden Books)
The Egg Book (1975, Macmillan)
Deck the Halls with Boughs of Holly (1975, Scholastic)
The Animobile Book (1976, Scholastic)
Jack Kent's Happy Ever After Book (1976, Random House)
Merry Mother Goose (1977, Golden Press)
The Funny Book (1977, Western)
Cindy Lou and the Witch's Dog (1978, Random House)
How Did They Get from Here to There When George Washington Was Young? (filmstrip; 1978, Scholastic)
Socks for Supper (1978, Parents' Magazine Press)
Supermarket Magic: A Sniffy Book (1978, Random House)
Piggy Bank Gonzales (1979, Parents' Magazine Press)

Floyd, the Tiniest Elephant (1979, Doubleday)
Hoddy Doddy (1979, Greenwillow)
Jack Kent's Hokus Pokus Bedtime Book (1979, Random House)
Knee-High Nina (1980, Doubleday)
Little Peep (1981, Prentice Hall)
The Biggest Shadow in the Zoo (1981, Parents' Magazine Press)
The Scribble Monster (1981, Harcourt Brace Jovanovich)
Jack Kent's Sticker Fun Drawing Book (1981, Scholastic)
The Once-Upon-a-Time Dragon (1982, Harcourt Brace Jovanovich)
Round Robin (1982, Prentice Hall)
The Caterpillar and the Polliwog (1982, Prentice Hall)
Jack Kent's Valentines Sticker Book (1982, Scholastic)
Silly Goose (1983, Prentice Hall)
Jim Jimmy James (1984, Greenwillow)
Joey (1984, Prentice Hall)
Joey Runs Away (1985, Prentice Hall)

As illustrator

Jack Kent's Book of Nursery Tales (Polly Berrien Berends, 1970, Random House)
The Bremen Town Musicians (Ruth Belov Gross, 1974, Scholastic)
How to Make Possum's Honey Bread . . . (Carla Stevens, 1975, Seabury Press)
I Was Walking Down the Road (Sarah Barchas, 1975, Scholastic)
The Magic Carrot Seeds (Carla Stevens, 1976, Scholastic)
Seven at One Blow (Freya Littledale, 1976, Scholastic)
Why Can't I Fly (Rita Goldman Gelman, 1976, Scholastic)
More Spaghetti, I Say (Rita Goldman Gelman, 1977, Scholastic)
The Emperor's New Clothes (Ruth Belov Gross, 1977, Four Winds)
Janie and the Giant (Sarah Barchas, 1977, Scholastic)
Tiny and Tony: A Golden Book of Picture Postcards (Seymour Reit, 1977, Golden Books)
The Simple Prince (Jane Yolen, 1978, Parents' Magazine Press)
Laura's Story (Beatrice Schenk de Regniers, 1979, Atheneum)
No One Noticed Ralph (Bonnie Bishop, 1979, Doubleday)
Ralph Rides Away (Bonnie Bishop, 1979, Doubleday)
Big Bear, Spare That Tree (Richard J. Margolis, 1980, Greenwillow)
If You Grew Up with George Washington (Ruth Belov Gross, 1982, Scholastic)
The Girl Who Wouldn't Get Married (Ruth Belov Gross, 1983, Four Winds)
Grime Doesn't Pay: Law and Order Jokes (Charles Keller, 1984, Prentice Hall)
Q Is for Duck (Michael Folsom and Mary Elting, 1985, Houghton Mifflin)
Easy as Pie: A Guessing Game of Sayings (Michael Folsom and Marcia Folsom, 1985,
    Houghton Mifflin)
The Twiddle Twins' Haunted House (Howard Goldsmith, 1985, Caedmon)

146   Appendix

Translations

Meneer Nosie (Dutch and Afrikaans translations of *Mr. Meebles* by Hannsie du
Toit, 1972)

Die Towenaar Van Tiekiedraai (Dutch and Afrikaans translations of *The Wizard of
Wallaby Way* by Hannsie du Toit, 1972)

*Füchschen Faxchen: Das große Geschichtenbuch für kleine Leute Gebundene von Jack
Kent* (German translation of *Jack Kent's Book of Nursery Tales*, 1973)

De Gamla Goda Sagorna (Swedish translation of *Jack Kent's Book of Nursery Tales*,
1975)

Wer Macht Dies Und Wer Macht Das? (German translation of *Jack Kent's Hop, Skip
and Jump Book*, 1976)

Matilda Muu (Swedish translation of *Mrs. Mooley* by Kaj Andersson, 1976)

Rouva Muu (Finnish translation of *Mrs. Mooley* by Panu Pekkanen, 1976)

Blommetjie En Die Maan (Afrikaans translation of *Mrs. Mooley* by Louise Steyn,
1976)

Julia und der Zauberhund (German translation of *Cindy Lou and the Witch's Dog*, 1976)

Les Deux Amis (French translation of *Tiny and Tony*, 1977)

Kurisumasu No Tsubo (Japanese translation of *The Christmas Piñata*, 1977)

De Kat Werd Hoe Langer Hoe Dikker: Een Oud Deens Sprookje (Dutch translation of
The Fat Cat by Frank Herzen, 1982)

Les Noces Du Fermier (French translation of *The Girl Who Wouldn't Get Married* by
Marianne Soffer Thomson, 1983)

Das Mädchen, Das Nicht Heiraten Wollte (German translation of *The Girl Who
Wouldn't Get Married* by Angelika Feilhauer, 1983)

Het Meisje Dat Niet Wilde Trouwen (Dutch translation of *The Girl Who Wouldn't Get
Married* by Frank Herzen, 1983)

Bête Comme Une Oie (French translation of *Silly Goose* by Catherine Deloraine, 1985)

Gachoⓧ To Kitsune (Japanese translation of *Silly Goose* by Hiroko Ishizawa, 1985)

Le Fermier et Sa Femme (French translation of "The Husband Who Tried to Keep
House," 1985)

Chiisana Pīpu (Japanese translation of *Little Peep* by Hiroko Ishizawa, 1985)

Jojo le Kangurou (French translation of *Joey* by Catherine Deloraine, 1986)

Paseba Por Un Caminito (Spanish translation of *I Was Walking Down the Road*, 1987)

Gros Rouge-Gorge (French translation of *Round Robin*, 1988)

Un Poussin Très Malin (French translation of *Little Peep*, 1988)

Chibikko Jōi (Japanese translation of *Joey* by Hiroko Ishizawa, 1988)

Jōi No Bōken (Japanese translation of *Joey Runs Away* by Hiroko Ishizawa, 1988)

Joey Part En Voyage (French translation of *Joey Runs Away*, 1988)

La Fille Qui Ne Voulait Pas Se Marier (French translation of *The Girl Who Wouldn't
Get Married*, 1994)

Kom, Kom, Så Skal I Bare Høre—: Den Ene Historie Efter Den Anden (Danish translation of *Jack Kent's Book of Nursery Tales* by Inge-Lise Hauerslev, 1996)

La Vache Qui Voulait Sauter Par-dessus la Lune (French translation of *Mrs. Mooley* by Rose-Marie Vassallo, 1996)

Dikouso Tsa Sijo Sa Bosigo (Tswana translation of *Socks for Supper* by Sidima Mntubu, 1996)

Futotcho neko: Denmāku minwa (Japanese translation of *The Fat Cat* by Akie Maezawa, 2001)

Drachen Gibt's Doch Gar Nicht (German translation of *There's No Such Thing as a Dragon* by Ute Andreson, 2004)

Les Dragons ça n'existe pas (French translation of *There's No Such Thing as a Dragon*, 2011)

Drakon—En Davar Ka-zeh (Hebrew translation of *There's No Such Thing as a Dragon* by Avraham Yavin, 2012)

Xiao Qiao Tao Pao Le (Chinese translation of *Joey Runs Away* by Hong-shu Chen, 2014)

Klotylda (Polish translation of *Clotilda* by Justyna Kluska, 2018)

Alternate Versions

The Wizard and His Magic Spells (1976, Reader's Digest)—Retitled version of *The Wizard of Wallaby Wallow*

The Fox and the Crow and 10 Other Tales (1976, Reader's Digest)—Abridged version of *Jack Kent's Fables of Aesop*

Clotilda's Magic (Scholastic paperback, 1978)—Retitled and colorized version of *Clotilda*

Audio/Visual Adaptations

Just Only John filmstrip produced by Look, Listen, & Learn, year unknown

Dooly and the Snortsnoot audio version produced by Ginn and Company, year unknown

The Blah filmstrip produced by Learning Corporation of America, 1972

The Bremen Town Musicians audio version produced by Scholastic Records, 1974

The Wizard of Wallaby Wallow audio version produced by Reader's Digest Services, 1976 (under the title *The Wizard and His Magic Spells*)

There's No Such Thing as a Dragon audio version produced by Disneyland Records, 1976

Seven at One Blow audio version produced by Scholastic, 1976

The Emperor's New Clothes audio version produced by Scholastic, 1978

How Did They Get from Here to There When George Washington Was Young? filmstrip produced by Scholastic, 1979

148 Appendix

The Wizard of Wallaby Wallow animated adaptation produced by Weston Woods, 1985 (under the title *The Wizard*)

Why Can't I Fly audio version produced by Scholastic, 1985

Mrs. Mooley animated adaptation by Golden Books Video, 1986

There's No Such Thing as a Dragon animated adaptation by Golden Books Video, 1986

Merry Mother Goose animated adaptation by Golden Books Video, 1986

I Was Walking Down the Road audio version by Scholastic, 1987

The Caterpillar and the Polliwog animated adaptation by Weston Woods, 1988

Joey Runs Away animated adaptation by Weston Woods, 1988

II. DEDICATIONS

Wizard of Wallaby Wallow—"To Tony"—Unknown.

Dooly and the Snortsnoot—"To John"—John Igo was an English professor at San Antonio College who published twelve books of poetry. He and Jack became friendly at Rosengren's Books; Jack also dedicated *The Caterpillar and the Polliwog* to Igo.

Jack Kent's Hop, Skip and Jump Book—"To Kevin, Kim, and Terry Lou"—Three of Jack's grand nephews and nieces (the first two Kent's children, the last Judy's daughter).

Hoddy Doddy—"To Honey and Wes"—Honey Raubolt was June's cousin on her mother's side. She and her husband Wes lived in Chicago for a long time.

Floyd, the Tiniest Elephant—"To Jenny and Jane and David"—Three more grand-nephews and -nieces (the first was Judy's second daughter, the second two Carter's children).

Jack Kent's Hokus Pokus Bedtime Book—"To the Fantastic KCRC and Margot"—This was Kent Cummins and his wife.

Little Peep—"To Judy and Don"—Jack's niece and her husband, Don Wonyetye.

Jim Jimmy James—"To Dawn and Sandy"—Unknown.

Silly Goose—"To Figgi and Cam"—Jack's friends from Rosengren's Books: Frank Rosengren Jr. and Camille Rosengren.

Knee-High Nina—"To Carter and Debbye"—Jack's nephew and his wife.

Joey—"To Naomi and Michael"—Jack and June's neighbors, Naomi Shihab Nye and her husband.

Joey Runs Away—"To Barbara"—Barbara Francis was Jack's editor at Prentice Hall.

Appendix

III. AUTHOR INFORMATION

Polly Berrien Berends
(*Jack Kent's Book of Nursery Tales*)

Polly Berrien Berends (1939–2107) was born in Chicago. She attended Skidmore College, Union Theological Seminary, and Columbia University. She worked as an editor for both Golden Press and Random House from 1963 to 1972 and published several children's books, including *The Case of the Elevator Duck* (1973) and *Ladybug, Dog, and the Night Walk* (1980). She also wrote books on parenting such as *Whole Child, Whole Parent* (1983) and *Gently Lead* (1992). In addition to writing, she was a sculptor and a pastoral counselor and had two sons, Jan and Andy. She wrote these words of wisdom: "Everything that happens to you is your teacher. The secret is to learn to sit at the feet of your own life and be taught by it."

• • •

Ruth Belov Gross
(*The Bremen Town Musicians, The Emperor's New Clothes, If You Grew Up with George Washington,* and *The Girl Who Wouldn't Get Married*)

Ruth Belov Gross was born in Philadelphia in 1929 and grew up in Florida. After graduating from the University of Miami, she headed to New York and became an editorial assistant working on children's books. She moved on to medical writing until publishing her first book in 1970, the nonfiction *What Do Animals Eat?* She hadn't planned to become an author, remarking, "I was finally doing what I had always wanted to do—without knowing that it was what I had always wanted to do." The many books that followed tended to be either nonfiction or retellings of traditional stories.

Ruth took a meticulous approach to her work, as evidenced by the fact that before writing her telling of *The Emperor's New Clothes*, she compared nine different versions of the story. She loved working with Jack and wrote to him upon his assignment to *The Emperor's New Clothes*, "I'm so happy to be having another Jack Kent book!"

• • •

Carla Stevens
(*How To Make Possum's Honey Bread . . . and The Magic Carrot Seeds*)

Carla Stevens Bigelow was born in 1928 in New York. She earned her bachelor's and master's degrees at New York University and then landed a job as an editor in

150 Appendix

the juvenile department of Addison-Wesley, where she worked from 1955 to 1969. During that time, she started her career as a children's writer with a series of books about a rabbit and a skunk illustrated by fellow children's author Robert Kraus. Her writing career continued simultaneously with her work as a teacher at the Dalton School in New York City. A strong believer in environmentalism, she was also a member of the board of trustees of Pratt Education Center. She published twenty books in all, in addition to teaching a popular class about keeping a diary at the New School for Social Research. She has one son and two daughters and lives in Cornwall, Connecticut.

• • •

Sarah Barchas
(*I Was Walking Down the Road* and *Janie and the Giant*)

Since she was young, Sarah Barchas has had a fascination with nature and animals. Her family had a cabin in the mountains, where she liked to catch insects and small animals. On one occasion, she caught three lizards and named them Liz, Lizzy, and Elizabeth. After a couple of days, she set them free. This experience clearly informed the idea for *I Was Walking Down the Road*, in which a little girl catches several different animals and places them in cages, only to let them all go at the end.

As is typical, Sarah had no say in who Scholastic assigned as an illustrator for her book, but she says that Jack Kent was the exact right choice. She says the final result is in "an absolutely perfect wedding of text and illustration" and "Nobody could have done it better than Jack Kent." A large part of her enthusiasm about the job he did arises from the way he injected his own sensibility into the story. "The layers that Jack Kent added, and additional dimensions to the original text were absolutely brilliant. They were charming, they extended, expanded, and enhanced the text. He was so imaginative and he had such a sense of humor."

The book sold over 750,000 copies, remained in print for several years, was produced as a "big book" for teachers, and was translated into Spanish (*Paseaba Por Un Caminito*). Most importantly, Sarah says, she has had many a person tell her that they learned to read from *I Was Walking Down the Road*.

Sarah's second book for Scholastic—a tale about a small girl bullied by a boastful giant—teamed her up with Jack again. For *Janie and the Giant*, the purpose was not about supporting and building reading skills but sending a message to children about finding their strengths. Her dedication reads: "For all girls, and boys, and grownups who try to solve giant problems."

The book wasn't as successful, sales- or longevity-wise, as *I Was Walking Down the Road*, but once again Sarah appreciated Jack's approach to the pictures, such as when the giant slices a large tree with a chop while Janie attacks a little flower. "He put himself into whatever he did," Sarah says of Jack.

• • •

Freya Littledale
(*Seven at One Blow*)

Freya Littledale (1929–1992) was born in New York into a family of musicians. She attended Ithaca College and New York University and taught English for one year before sliding over to editing. She worked as an editor for twelve years, including a stint at Parents' Magazine Press. Her books were largely adaptations of fairy tales and traditional stories. "I think of my books as long poems in story form," she said. "Each word is chosen as carefully as the polished stones I collect." Appropriately, in 1979 she released a poetry collection called *I Was Thinking*, with illustrations by Leonard Kessler.

• • •

Rita Golden Gelman
(*Why Can't I Fly* and *Spaghetti for Supper*)

Rita Goldman Gelman was born in 1937 in Bridgeport, Connecticut. She attended Brandeis University and became an editor in the 1960s. She published her first book, *Dumb Joey*, in 1973 (with illustrator Cheryl Pelavin), kicking off a prolific career writing for children. In 1986 living in Los Angeles at age forty-eight, her kids grown and on the verge of divorce, she decided to try a different way of life and became nomadic. She got rid of most of her possessions and began traveling all over the world, rarely planning much more than six months ahead and letting serendipity guide her. She wrote a book about the experience, *Tales of a Female Nomad*, which was published by Crown in 2001.

Her favorite book of the over seventy she's had published is *Why Can't I Fly*. Rita says the story "comes from the part of me that used to lie in the grass as a child and watch the birds. I still dream about flying, soaring, riding the wind." She likes that the book is about doing the impossible, which she describes as "a pretty relative thing." She goes on, "What is impossible for one person, may be quite possible for someone else. A lot depends on how hard you try and how capable you are of listening to the voice inside your head instead of the voices outside. Much of the time, a little flexibility and a lot of will, can make the impossible happen."

• • •

Seymour Reit
(*Tiny and Tony*)

Seymour Reit (1918–2001) was born in New York City and attended New York College. Right out of school, he moved to Miami and worked for Fleischer Studios as both an artist and a gag writer for *Betty Boop* and *Popeye* cartoons. He eventually transitioned into creating comic strips and comic books for shops run by Jerry Iger and Will Eisner. It was during this time that he and artist Joe Oriolo collaborated to create a character they called Caspar the Friendly Ghost. They sold the rights to the idea to Famous Studios for $200. Caspar, of course, went on to become world famous.

After World War II, during which Reit worked painting scenes designed to disguise potential targets on the West Coast, he returned to animation and comics, writing screenplays for Caspar shorts, drawing *Archie* and *Little Lulu*, and landing steady work at *Mad Magazine*. He worked on *Captain Kangaroo* and with the Bank Street College of Education. He began writing books too, building a journeyman's career with more than eighty titles to his name, ranging from nonfiction histories to *Bugs Bunny Goes to the Dentist*.

• • •

Jane Yolen
(*The Simple Prince*)

Jane Yolen (born 1939) is an amazingly prolific writer (386 books and counting) who has won many awards and has had her books illustrated by the likes of Mark Teague, Mercer Mayer, James Marshall, and Tomie DePaola. She was born in New York, grew up at least in part in Connecticut, and graduated Smith College in 1960. She worked as an editor until the mid-1960s, when she published her first book, *The Witch Who Wasn't*. Contemporary Authors wrote, "Yolen is perhaps best known for creating original folk and fairy tales and fables that contain a surprising twist and a strong moral core."

• • •

Bonnie Bishop
(*No One Noticed Ralph* and *Ralph Rides Away*)

Bonnie Bishop was born in 1943 in Meridian, Connecticut. She attended Skidmore College for her undergraduate degree, got her MFA from Syracuse, and attended Parsons School for Design. She worked as an artist and art editor for Scholastic for several years. Her only two books as an author were *No One Noticed Ralph* and *Ralph Rides Away*, both published in 1979. In 1985 she illustrated Doris Gove's *Miracle at Egg Rock: A Puffin's Story*. That was followed in 1998 by Kate Rowinski's *Cats in the Dark*. By this time Bonnie had settled in Maine, where she worked for Colby College. Over the years, she has spread her expertise and love of papermaking and book art by teaching at several different institutions and offering workshops in her studio.

• • •

Appendix   153

Beatrice Shenk de Regniers
(*Laura's Story*)

Beatrice Schenk de Regniers (1914–2000) was born in Lafayette, Indiana. She attended the University of Illinois and the University of Chicago before heading east to New York. She became a copywriter and then started to sell her children's book manuscripts. This resulted in two books with a prefame Maurice Sendak (1953's *The Giant Story* and 1955's *What Can You Do with a Shoe?*), a Caldecott in 1965, and nearly fifty total published books. She worked as an editor for Scholastic's Lucky Book Club from 1961 to 1981. She said, "I think of writing—particularly of writing picture books—as a kind of choreography. A picture book must have pace and movement and pattern. Pictures and text should, together, create the pattern, rather than simply run parallel."

• • •

Richard J. Margolis
(*Big Bear, Spare That Tree!*)

Richard J. Margolis (1929–1991) was born in Saint Paul, Minnesota. He attended the University of Minnesota, earning his master's degree. He started out as a journalist, eventually landing work in *Life*, the *Smithsonian Magazine*, the *New Republic*, the *New York Times Magazine*, and *Harper's*. He began writing a column in the *New Leader* highlighting social issues, with a special interest in marginalized groups, such as migrant workers, the rural poor, immigrants, Native Americans, and the elderly.

Margolis published his first book for children in 1968, a collection of poems called *Only the Moon and Me*. Several more followed, as did books for adults. The Richard J. Margolis Award is now given annually to up-and-coming journalists/essayists whose work "combines warmth, humor and wisdom and sheds light on issues of social justice."

• • •

Charles Keller
(*Grime and Punishment: Law and Order Jokes*)

Charles Keller (1932–2001) was born in New York but spent much of his life in New Jersey. He attended St. Peter's University in Jersey City, New Jersey, and entered a career in comedy. In the 1970s he worked as a script consultant for CBS, contributing to hit shows such as *M*A*S*H*, *All in the Family*, and *The Mary Tyler Moore Show*. Somewhere along the way he began to collect children's riddles, jokes, and rhymes and, unhappy with the state of children's joke books, began

154   Appendix

writing his own. He started in 1973 with *Ballpoint Bananas and Other Jokes for Kids*, and after that his published oeuvre grew to over fifty joke books, including such titles as *Alexander the Grape: Fruit and Vegetable Jokes* and *Colossal Fossils: Dinosaur Riddles* (1987). He also published the anthologies *Laughing: A Historical Selection of American Humor* in 1977 and *Growing Up Laughing: Humorists Look at American Youth* in 1981.

• • •

Michael Folsom, Mary Elting, and Marcia Folsom
(*Q Is for Duck* and *Easy as Pie*)

Michael Folsom (1938–1990) cowrote two books that Jack illustrated, one with his mother and the other with his wife. Writing was clearly a family business.

Michael's mother, Mary Elting (1906–2005) was born in Creede, Colorado, and attended college at the University of Colorado. After graduation, she headed to New York, landing a job as a secretary at *Forum Magazine*. She was made a copyeditor after a week. In the mid-1930s, Mary married Franklin Folsom, whom she had met her sophomore year at university. After graduating, he taught two years at Swarthmore College and then spent three more at Oxford as a Rhodes Scholar before joining Mary in New York.

Both Mary and Franklin were social activists and members of the Communist Party and were passionate about antifascism and equal rights. This is ironic because many of Mary's early nonfiction books for children were on the topics of war and government. Her first, published in 1943, was *Soldiers, Sailors, Fliers, and Marines*. She published over forty books in her career, the majority nonfiction, and several under male pseudonyms such as Campbell Tatham and Davis Cole. Franklin began writing for children too, and the couple cowrote 1960's *The Story of Archeology in the Americas*.

Mary and Franklin had two children, Michael and Rachel. Rachel attended Swarthmore College and became a painter. She cowrote one book with her mother, *Volcanos and Earthquakes* (Simon and Schuster, 1990). Michael was born in New York. He attended Antioch College, Rutgers, and the University of California–Berkley, where he earned a PhD in English. He taught for several years at the Massachusetts Institute of Technology in a variety of subject areas. In 1980 he cofounded the Charles River Museum of Industry and served for many years as its first director. He wrote three other books with his mother, *The Secret Story of Pueblo Bonito* (1963), *The Mysterious Grain* (1967), and *The Answer Book about Robots and Other Inventions* (1984). He said his two sons' love of riddles partly inspired *Q Is for Duck*.

Michael met Marcia at Berkeley, and the two married in 1967. She was born Marcia McClintock in 1940 and had attended Wellesley College before heading to Berkeley to work on her master's degree. She eventually completed her PhD, also at Berkeley. In 1986 she began teaching literature at Wheelock College in Boston and has been there ever since, serving currently as Chair of Humanities and Writing. She is well known as an expert on the works of Jane Austen. In addition to *Easy as Pie*, she and Michael coauthored *The Macmillan Book of How Things Work* (1987). She has since served as editor of *Approaches to Teaching Austen's* Pride and Prejudice (1993), *Approaches to Teaching Austen's* Emma (2004), and *Approaches to Teaching Austen's* Mansfield Park (2014).

• • •

Howard Goldsmith
(*The Twiddle Twins' Haunted House*)

Howard Goldsmith (1943–2011) was born in New York and graduated from the University of New York. He was an Arthur Rackham predoctoral fellow at the University of Michigan, and he earned a master's degree in psychology. He published his first book, *Turvey, the Horse That Ran Backward* in 1973 and went on to author more than sixty books and many short stories. He had a special interest in science fiction, writing *Terror by Night, and Other Strange Tales* (1977) and *Invasion: 2200 A.D.* (1979), and also wrote many books for early readers. While writing, he also worked as an editor at various publishers, including Santillana and Children's Magic Window. He called it "especially gratifying" to have Jack illustrate *The Twiddle Twins' Haunted House*. He went on to create three more books about the characters with illustrator Charles Jordan.

IV. JACK KENT'S OTHER PUBLISHED WORK

King Aroo
King Aroo. Doubleday, 1953.
A Private Gem in a Public Setting: An Original Commentary on Education by Some of America's Leading Cartoonists. New College Foundation, 1978.
King Aroo: 1950–1952. IDW Publishing, 2010.
King Aroo: 1952–1954. IDW Publishing, 2013.

Cartoons

Playboy, Jul. 1967.
Parade, 9 Jul. 1967.

156   Appendix

Parade, 22 Oct. 1967.

Parade, 12 Nov. 1967.

Parade, 24 Dec. 1967.

Playboy, Mar. 1968.

Saturday Evening Post, 20 Apr. 1968.

Saturday Evening Post, 29 Jun. 1968.

Saturday Evening Post, 27 Jul. 1968.

Saturday Evening Post, 21 Sep. 1968.

"Why Christmas Almost Wasn't." Nationally syndicated in newspapers, Dec. 1968.

Saturday Evening Post, 28 Dec. 1968.

"A MAD Look at Sex Education in the Schools." *Mad Magazine*, no. 125, Mar. 1969.

"A MAD Look at Frustration" (with Paul Coker Jr.). *Mad Magazine*, no. 126, Apr. 1969.

"You Know You're Really Overweight When" (with Paul Coker Jr.). *Mad Magazine*, no. 128, Jul. 1969.

"You Know You're Really a Nobody When." (with Paul Coker Jr.). *Mad Magazine*, no. 130, Oct. 1969.

"Knight-fall" (with Jack Rickard). *Mad Magazine*, no. 132, Jan. 1970.

"You're an Eternal Optimist If" (with Tom Koch and Jack Davis). *Mad Magazine*, no. 194, Oct. 1977.

Short stories and poems

"Puppies" (with Jack Kent Jr.). *Humpty Dumpty's Magazine for Little Children*, Oct. 1967.

"Oscar." *Humpty Dumpty's Magazine for Little Children*, Jan. 1970.

"Lovely Day." *Humpty Dumpty's Magazine for Little Children*, Feb. 1970.

"Toggle." *Humpty Dumpty's Magazine for Little Children*, Mar. 1970.

"The Lonely Tree." *Humpty Dumpty's Magazine for Little Children*, Apr. 1970.

"The Wonderful Magic Spell." *Humpty Dumpty's Magazine for Little Children*, Nov. 1970.

"The Runaway." *Humpty Dumpty's Magazine for Little Children*, Jan. 1971.

"All the Answers." *Humpty Dumpty's Magazine for Little Children*, Feb. 1971.

"Nobody." *Humpty Dumpty's Magazine for Little Children*, Apr. 1971.

Cover illustration. *Humpty Dumpty's Magazine for Little Children*, May 1971.

"The Birdhouse." *Humpty Dumpty's Magazine for Little Children*, Jul. 1971.

Cover illustration. *Humpty Dumpty's Magazine for Little Children*, Sep. 1971.

"The Kite." *Humpty Dumpty's Magazine for Little Children*, Sep. 1971.

"The Butterfly." *Humpty Dumpty's Magazine for Little Children*, Oct. 1971.

"The Watchdog." *Humpty Dumpty's Magazine for Little Children*, Nov. 1971.

Cover illustration. *Humpty Dumpty's Magazine for Little Children*, Jan. 1972.

"King Norton the Nasty." *Humpty Dumpty's Magazine for Little Children*, Jan. 1972.

"Let's Be Frogs." *Humpty Dumpty's Magazine for Little Children*, Apr. 1972.

"Aesop's Fables." *Humpty Dumpty's Magazine for Little Children*, Jul. 1972.

"Meet Jack Kent." *Give Me a Clue*. Ginn & Company, 1985.

"An Old Kitten is a Cat." *Give Me a Clue*. Ginn & Company, 1985.

"The Early Bird." *Ladybug*, Oct. 1998.

"The Firefly" (with Susan Estelle Kwas). *Cricket*, vol. 35, no. 11 Jul. 2005.

Notes

Front Matter Epigraph

"share with you": Jack Kent, "Meet Jack Kent." *Give Me a Clue*, edited by Theodore Clymer. Ginn and Company, 1985, p. 42.

Chapter 1: From Pillar to Post (1920–1936)

4   "kitty mows": Jane M., "Jack Kent Went from Comic Strips to Children's Books." Austin American-Statesman, 31 Aug. 1979.

6   "we moved": Jack Kent, *Fifth Book of Junior Authors and Illustrators*, edited by Sally Holmes Holtze, T. H. Wilson, 1983, p. 171.

6   "fancy-free": Bruce Canwell, "Titanic Tales of a Talented Texan: The Road to Myopia." *King Aroo: Daily and Sunday Comics 1950–1952*. IDW Publishing, 2010, p. 12.

6   "four-to-six": Jack Kent Jr. Interview with Paul V. Allen, 21 Jul. 2020.

8   "life satisfaction": Shigehiro Oishi and Ulrich Schimmak, "Residential Mobility, Well-Being, and Mortality." *Journal of Personality and Social Psychology*, vol. 98, no. 6, 2010, pp. 980–94.

8   "for whom": Ron White, "Jack Kent: Just a Kid at Heart." *San Antonio Express Sunday Magazine*, 23 Jun. 1974.

8   "my first great love": Jack Kent to Karen O'Connell, 15 Dec. 1984.

8   "medium is an art": John Wellington Kent. Gale Literature: Contemporary Authors, 2020. Gale in Context: Biography. Document number: GALE H1080048707, 21 Jan. 1985 interview.

10   "gave it up": *Fifth Book*, p. 171.

Notes 159

Chapter 2: "Texas Jack" (1937–1941)

13   "that looks stupid": Jack Kent Jr. Interview with PVA, 21 Jul. 2020.

14   "proper definition": John Wellington Kent. Gale Literature: Contemporary Authors, 2020. Gale in Context: Biography. Document number: GALE H1080048707, 21 Jan. 1985 interview.

15   "learned more": Jack Kent to Karen O'Connell, 15 Dec. 1984.

16   "embarrassing stereotype": Mark Carlson-Ghost, "Big Chief Wahoo and Race in Comic Strips." www.markcarlson-ghost.com. 28 Dec. 2019. https://www.markcarlson-ghost.com/index.php/2019/12/28/big-chief-wahoo/.

Chapter 3: Tedious Business (1942–1949)

17   "Herriman blushed": Jack Kent to Karen O'Connell, 15 Dec. 1984.

19   "court-martial you": Jack Kent Jr. Interview with Paul V. Allen, 21 Jul. 2020.

21   "I'm leaving": Jack Kent Jr. Interview with Paul V. Allen, 21 Jul. 2020.

21   "nothing left": ibid.

22   "what I could": John Wellington Kent, Gale Literature: Contemporary Authors, 2020. Gale in Context: Biography. Document number: GALE H1080048707, 21 Jan. 1985 interview.

22   "skip stones": Jack Kent Jr., "Jack Kent, King Aroo, and King William." King William Association. History—People. 2010. https://www.ourkwa.org/articles/history-people/422-jack-kent-king-aroo-and-king-william.

Chapter 4: Willywampusses Are Chasing Geezles (1950)

23   "dancing antistrophe": "King Aroo's Creator Lives on Whimsical Adventures." *Pasadena Independent*, 1 Jul. 1955.

23   "full entourage": ibid.

24   "get a job": Selby Kelly and Bill Crouch Jr., editors, *The Best of Pogo*. Fireside, 1982, p. 155.

24   "VERY BRIEF": Canwell, 2010, p. 23.

24   "chasing geezles": ibid.

26   "fantasy and whimsey": "King Aroo Makes Debut." *Times Colonist*, 20 Nov. 1950.

27   "That's only seven!": *King Aroo*, 15 Dec. 1950.

28   "bourgeois": *King Aroo*, 24 Dec. 1950.

Chapter 5: Love Is Ageless, Deathless . . .
and Penniless (1951–1953)

29 "counting your money": Canwell, 2013, p. 6.

30 "picturesque blonde": "Western Girl Went West to Gain Singing Success." *The Charlotte News*, 21 Nov. 1951.

31 "He's serious": *King Aroo*, 22 Jul. 1951.

32 "Betelgeuse": *King Aroo*, 5 Apr. 1954.

32 "hare from it": *King Aroo*, 21 Jan. 1951.

32 "high school": *King Aroo*, 8 Oct. 1951.

32 "cheap wit": *King Aroo*, 29 Dec. 1950.

33 "really worthwhile": *King Aroo*, 7 Apr. 1962.

33 "air raid siren": *King Aroo*, 18 Oct. 1952.

33 "dogged his footsteps": *King Aroo*, 30 May 1954.

33 "Pop!": *King Aroo*, 4 Nov. 1951.

33 "Cheektowaga": *King Aroo*, 21 Nov. 1950.

35 "glamorous": "Royal Comic Strip." *People Today*, 25 Feb. 1953.

37 "seven days a week": Gale, 1985.

37 "worse than death": Sidney Fields, "Hooked on Fishing." *New York Daily News*, 15 Jan. 1966.

38 "too lonely": *King Aroo*, 20 Apr. 1963.

Chapter 6: Junie and Jack Jr. (1953–1957)

40 "logic of its own": Gilbert Seldes, "Introduction." *King Aroo*. Doubleday, 1953, p. 6.

40 "specific marks": ibid.

41 "a warning": Jack Kent to Karen O'Connell, 15 Dec. 1984.

42 "come back later": *King Aroo*, 17 Oct. 1953.

43 "leave a note": *King Aroo*, 9 Aug. 1953.

43 "applesauce": *King Aroo*, 27 Jun. 1953.

46 "for a bride": Tom Devlin, "All Hail Jack Kent!" *The Comics Journal Special Edition*, vol. 2, summer 2002, p. 6.

47 "lovely garden": Canwell, 2013, p. 10.

48 "hooked for life": Monte Roberts, "Between Times." *Times Colonist* (Victoria, BC), 4 Nov. 1953.

48 "actually comic": Monte Roberts, "Between Times." *Times Colonist* (Victoria, BC), 21 Jul. 1955.

48 "at his best": "As Our Readers See It." *Times Colonist*, 22 May 1956, p. 4.

Notes 161

Chapter 7: My Future Looks Rosy, but Not Very Big! (1957–1960)

51   "'fess up": *King Aroo*, 15 Dec. 1950.

51   "Athens Daily Bugle": *King Aroo*, 6 May 1951.

52   "out here": *King Aroo*, 13 Apr. 1953.

52   "our ancestors": *King Aroo*, 28 Nov. 1953.

52   "back to the plot": *King Aroo*, 2 Apr. 1952.

52   "blew up": *King Aroo*, 1 Mar. 1957.

53   "building permit": *King Aroo*, 8 Mar. 1957.

55   "tucked behind": Jack Kent Jr., "Jack Kent's Home & Work." *Vintage Children's Books My Kid Loves*, 11 Feb. 2010.

55   "bohemian and intimate": ibid.

Chapter 8: Illogical Conclusions (1960–1965)

59   "instant puddings": *King Aroo*, 3 Oct. 1954.

59   "being extinct": *King Aroo*, 14 Sep. 1963.

59   "bloody battle": *King Aroo*, 1 Jan. 1951.

59   "violence and conflict": *King Aroo*, 2 Apr. 1964.

61   "uncommon sweetness": Seldes, p. 8.

62   "infantile expressions": *King Aroo*, 18 Sep. 1953.

62   "month of drawing": Leslie Monypenny, "*King Aroo*'s Wit Flows from Pen of Zany Genius." *Chicago Tribune*, 31 Mar. 1952, p. 23.

63   "quality and talent": *King Aroo*, 3 Jul. 1963.

63   "saw how old": Canwell, 2013, p. 15.

Chapter 9: From *Humpty Dumpty* to *Playboy* (1965–1968)

67   "no excuses": Burgin Streetman, "Just Only Jack." *San Antonio Current*, 10 Feb. 2010.

68   "being unemployed": Gale, 1985.

69   "mind is closed": June Kent, "For Expo—Go!" *San Antonio Express*, 2 Jul. 1967.

71   "goodness knows": Jack Kent Jr. to Paul V. Allen (via email). 27 Oct. 2020.

72   "in the family": Jack Kent, *The Once-Upon-a-Time Dragon*. Harcourt Brace Jovanovich, 1982.

72   "in the country": Jack Kent. *Dooly and the Snortsnoot*. Putnam, 1972.

162 Notes

73   "tender and simpatico": Sergio Aragonés, "Introduction." *King Aroo, Daily and Sunday Comics 1950–1952*, p. 5.

74   "many leftovers": Jack Kent, "The Christmas That Almost Wasn't." 24 Dec. 1968.

Chapter 10: The Sandbox Set (1968–1970)

76   "look rational": John Wellington Kent, Gale Literature: Contemporary Authors, 2020. Gale in Context: Biography. Document number: GALE H1080048707, 21 Jan. 1985 interview.

76   "for their graphics": Jack Kent, "Graphics for Youths" *San Antonio Express*. 27 Sep. 1970.

77   "light whimsy": John Wellington Kent, Gale Literature: Contemporary Authors, 2020. Gale in Context: Biography. Document number: GALE H1080048707, 21 Jan. 1985 interview.

77   "crisply captured": Patricia Hall, "Johnny Gruelle, Creator of Raggedy Ann and Andy." Pelican, 1993, p. 19.

79   "wanted all along": Canwell, 2013, p. 17 (from Marjorie George article in *San Antonio Light or Express*?).

80   "flabbergasted": Jane M., "Jack Kent Went from Comic Strips to Children's Books." *Austin American-Statesman*, 31 Aug. 1979.

83   "in my mind": Gale, 1985.

83   "ought to be used": Gale, 1985.

Chapter 11: A Cartoonist at Heart (1971–1974)

88   "cartoonist at heart": Canwell, 2013, p. 18.

88   "destiny": Jack Kent, *Floyd the Tiniest Elephant*. Doubleday, 1979.

88   "market for it": Gale, 1985.

96   "Danish and Swedish": ibid.

98   "alive and marvelous": Eve Lynn Sawyer, "Educational Tour Turns to Pleasure Trip." *San Antonio Express*, 27 Nov. 1974.

Chapter 12: Fringe Benefits (1975–1979)

99   "draw the pictures": *North San Antonio Times*, 3 Feb. 1977 (Canwell, 2013, p. 18).

Notes   163

99   "I was horrified": Gale, 1985.

100   "ridiculous": ibid.

103   "fringe benefit": "Jack Kent." Children's Book Art at the Contemporary Arts Museum (exhibit catalog). 8–30 Nov. 1975. Contemporary Arts Museum Houston.

107   "make me happy": Jack Kent to Susan Hirschman, 1 Mar. 1975. "Greenwillow Books Records." University of Oregon Libraries, Special Collections and University Archives.

107   "rare combination": Susan Hirschman to Paul V. Allen (via email), 18 Feb. 2021.

Chapter 13: No Great Genius (1980–1983)

111   "excuses nothing": Fifth Book, 171

111   "prove the rule": *King Aroo*, 29 Jul. 1951.

112   "no great genius": Gale, 1985.

113   "your frequency": Jack Kent to Susan Hirschman, 24 Oct. 1979. "Greenwillow Books Records." University of Oregon Libraries, Special Collections and University Archives.

114   "TV vulgar": Natalie Babbitt, "Children's Books." *New York Times*, 25 Sep. 1977, p. 273.

114   "wordless pages": Dana Whitney Pinizzotto, "The Scribble Monster." *School Library Journal*, vol. 28, no. 3, 1981, p. 78.

114   "new cities": Jack Kent Jr. to Paul V. Allen (via email). 27 Oct. 2020.

117   "public swimming pool": Gale, 1985.

Chapter 14: Just Only Jack (1984–1985)

118   "involved in work": Gale, 1985.

118   "nigh impossible": Fifth Book, p. 172.

118   "another book sometime": "Kent, John Wellington (Jack Kent)." *Something about the Author*, edited by Anne Commire. Gale, 1981.

118   "weightier fare": Fifth Book, p. 172.

119   "close to martyrdom": "Jack Kent, King Aroo, and King William." King William Association. History—People. 2010. https://www.ourkwa.org/articles/history-people/422-jack-kent-king-aroo-and-king-william.

121   "wonder and pleasure": "Kent, John Wellington (Jack Kent)." *Something about the Author,* edited by Anne Commire. Gale, 1981.

164 Notes

121 "beauty and creativity": "The People of St. Mark's Welcome You!" St. Mark's Episcopal Church Official Site. 2021. https://www.stmarks-sa .org/im-new/.

121 "outward stimulation": Naomi Shihab Nye. Interview with Paul V. Allen, 14 Feb. 2021.

121 "sweep your floors": ibid.

122 "Jack Kent the hermit": ibid.

122 "three of us": ibid.

122 "kind of guy": ibid.

124 "best recipient": ibid.

128 "something like this": Fifth Book, p. 172.

128 "summer and fall": Jack Kent Jr. Interview with Paul V. Allen, 21 Jul. 2020.

129 "whole neighborhood": Naomi Shihab Nye, "Rain Falling into the River— That Moment as They Merge." *Mint*. State Street Press Chapbooks, 1991.

Epilogue: Ever After (1986 and Beyond)

133 "complete with princess": Canwell, 2013, p. 21.

133 "ever offered": Kent Cummins, Interview with Paul V. Allen, 22 Jun. 2020.

134 "again and again": Shaenon Garrity, "The Strangest Pictures I Have Seen #6." *The Comics Journal* Blog. https://web.archive.org/web/20100712100854/ http://www.tcj.com/blog/the-strangest-pictures-i-have-seen-6.

135 "mind of a child": Jack Kent Jr. to Paul V. Allen (via email), 27 Oct. 2020.

137 "illogical conclusion": Christopher Finch, *Of Muppets and Men*. Alfred Knopf, 1981, p. 31.

137 "various categories": *The World Encyclopedia of Comics*. Edited by Maurice Horn. Chelsea House, 1976.

137 "devotees of comics": Bill Blackbeard and Martin Williams, editors, *The Smithsonian Collection of Newspaper Comics*. Smithsonian Institution Press and Harry N. Abrams, 1977, p. 330.

137 "visual charm": Dennis Wepman, "Kent, John Wellington (Jack Kent)." *Contemporary Graphic Artists*, vol. 1, edited by Maurice Horn. Gale Research, 1986, p. 160.

138 "flawless composition": Richard Marschall, "God Save the King!" *Nemo: The Classic Comics Library*, no. 21, Aug. 1986, p. 6.

138 "never flagged": Maurice Horn, *100 Years of American Newspaper Comics*. Random House, 1996

138 "giggling away": Tom Devlin, "All Hail Jack Kent!" *The Comics Journal Special Edition*, vol. 2, summer, 2002, p. 29.

Notes   165

138   "someday soon": Tom Evanier, "Sergio Sez." *News from Me*, 29 Dec. 2005.

139   "disappear forever": Streetman, "Just Only Jack."

140   "in comfort": Naomi Shihab Nye, Interview with Paul V. Allen, 14 Feb. 2021.

140   "got it wrong": Naomi Shihab Nye to Paul V. Allen (via email), 18 Dec. 2020.

141   "interview me": Fifth Book, p. 172.

141   "what I did": Jack Kent Jr. Interview with Paul V. Allen, 21 Jul. 2020.

142   "through-and-through": Naomi Shihab Nye, Interview with Paul V. Allen, 14 Feb. 2021.

Appendix

149   "taught by it": Polly Berrien Berends, *New York Times,* 19 Feb. 2017.

149   "always wanted to do": Ruth Belov Gross, Scholastic.com. https://www.scholastic.com/teachers/authors/ruth-belov-gross/. Accessed 18 Apr. 2020.

149   "having another": Ruth Belov Gross to Jack Kent. Undated. Jack Kent Papers, Kerlan Collection, MF1407, Miscellaneous Items folder 1.

150   "absolutely brilliant": Sarah Barchas, Interview with Paul V. Allen via phone, 7 May 2020.

151   "riding the wind": "Rita Golden Gelman." Gale, 2006. https://link-gale.com.ezproxy.ramsey.lib.mn.us/apps/doc/H1000035911/CA?u=ramsey_main&sid=CA&xid=1843789d. Accessed 17 Apr. 2020.

152   "strong moral core": "Jane Yolen." Gale Literature: Contemporary Authors, 2018. https://link-gale-com.ezproxy.ramsey.lib.mn.us/apps/doc/H1000108941/CA?u=ramsey_main&sid=CA&xid=e84eba5d. Accessed 17 Apr. 2020.

153   "run parallel": "Beatrice Schenk (Freedman) de Regniers." Gale Literature: Contemporary Authors, 2001. https://link-gale-com.ezproxy.ramsey.lib.mn.us/apps/doc/H1000024900/CA?u=ramsey_main&sid=CA&xid=fd0d117f. Accessed 17 Apr. 2020.

153   "social justice:" "Richard J. Margolis Award." https://www.margolisaward.org/. 2018. Accessed 18 Jun. 2020.

155   "especially gratifying": "Howard Goldsmith." Gale Literature: Contemporary Authors. 2012. https://link-gale-com.ezproxy.ramsey.lib.mn.us/apps/doc/H1000037703/CA?u=ramsey_main&sid=CA&xid=1f706b2c. Accessed 17 Apr. 2020.

References

Albanesi, Melanie. "Get a Closer Look at This Original Comic Collection." *Antiques Roadshow.* (PBS.org). 27 Apr. 2020. https://www.pbs.org/wgbh/roadshow/stories/articles/2020/4/27/get-closer-look-original-comic-collection. Accessed 28 May 2020.

Aragonés, Sergio. "Introduction." *King Aroo, Daily and Sunday Comics 1950–1952.* Library of American Comics, 2010, p. 5.

"Arts and Letters." *Friends of San Antonio Public Library.* http://www.friendsofsapl.org/arts—letters-awards.html. Accessed 20 Apr. 2020.

Babbitt, Natalie. "Children's Books." *New York Times,* 25 Sep. 1977, p. 273.

"Bataan Death March." History.com. 7 Jun. 2019. https://www.history.com/topics/world-war-ii/bataan-death-march. Accessed 29 Apr. 2020.

Beavin, Kristi Thomas. "Silly Goose." *School Library Journal,* vol. 30, no 1, 1983, p. 108.

Bevington, Helen. "Once Upon a Time and Ever After." *New York Times,* 14 Nov. 1976, p. 260.

Bishop, Rudine Sims. "Mirrors, Windows, and Sliding Glass Doors." *Perspectives: Choosing and Using Books for the Classroom,* vol. 6, no. 3, 1990, pp. 9–11.

Blackbeard, Bill, and Williams, Martin, editors. *The Smithsonian Collection of Newspaper Comics.* Smithsonian Institution Press and Harry N. Abrams, 1977, pp. 314–17.

"Bonnie Bishop." Gale. 2012. https://link-gale-com.ezproxy.ramsey.lib.mn.us/apps/doc/H1000008844/CA?u=ramsey_main&sid=CA&xid=df4a6d90. Accessed 17 Apr. 2020.

"Bonnie Bishop." *Maine Arts Commission.* https://mainearts.maine.gov/directory/arts/detail/135. Accessed 17 Jun. 2020.

Bowman, James H. "Don't Be a Fish." *The Herald* (Jasper, IN), 29 Dec. 1956.

Canwell, Bruce. "Titanic Tales of a Talented Texan: The Road to Myopia." *King Aroo: Daily and Sunday Comics 1950–1952.* Library of American Comics, 2010, pp. 5–25.

Canwell, Bruce. "Titanic Tales of a Talented Texan: Holding Court in King Aroo's Castle." *King Aroo: Daily and Sunday Comics 1952–1954.* Library of American Comics, 2013, pp. 5–21.

Canwell, Bruce. "A Few of My Favorite Things (Part I of II)." Library of American Comics. 3 May 2016. http://loac.idwpublishing.com/a-few-of-my-favorite-things-part-i-of-ii/. Accessed 15 May 2020.

References

"Carla McBride Stevens." *Gale Literature: Contemporary Authors. Gale Literature: Contemporary Authors.* 2009. https://link-gale-com.ezproxy.ramsey.lib.mn.us/apps/doc/H1000095046/CA?u=ramsey_main&sid=CA&xid=eec6cc73. Accessed 17 Apr. 2020.

Castillo, Lisa. "The Caterpillar and the Polliwog." *School Library Journal*, vol. 29, no. 5, 1983, p. 62.

"Charles Keller." Gale Literature: Contemporary Authors. 2012. https://link-gale-com.ezproxy.ramsey.lib.mn.us/apps/doc/H1000052977/BIC?u=ramsey_main&sid=BIC&xid=56a33328. Accessed 19 Jun. 2020.

Coley, Rebekah Levine, and Melissa Kull, "Cumulative, Timing-Specific, and Interactive Models of Residential Mobility and Children's Cognitive and Psychosocial Skills," *Child Development*, vol. 87, Jul–Aug 2016, pp. 1–17.

Commire, Anne, editor. "Kent, John Wellington (Jack Kent)." *Something about the Author.* Volume 24. Gale, 1981, pp. 135–37.

"Crab Grass." *School Library Journal*, vol. 28, no. 4, 1981, p. 77.

"Creator of 'King Aroo' Comic Speaks Eskimo and Owns Circle-Bar-K Brand, but No Cattle." *The News*, 10 Jun. 1954, p. 6.

Devlin, Tom. "All Hail Jack Kent!" *The Comics Journal Special Edition*, vol. 2, summer, 2002, pp. 24–37.

Diehl, Suzanne. "'Just Only John' Delightful Reading." *San Antonio Express*, 8 Sep. 1968.

Diehl, Suzanne. "Whimsy for Young Readers." *San Antonio Express,* 16 Nov. 1969.

Evanier, Mark. "Sergio Sez" *News from ME.* 29 Dec. 2005. https://www.newsfromme.com/2005/12/29/sergio-sez/. Accessed 4 Jun. 2020.

Fields, Sidney. "Hooked on Fishing." *New York Daily News*, 15 Jan. 1966.

"Freya (Lota) Littledale." Gale. 2001. https://link-gale-com.ezproxy.ramsey.lib.mn.us/apps/doc/H1000060608/CA?u=ramsey_main&sid=CA&xid=e26ecc31. Accessed 17 Apr. 2020.

Gelman, Rita Golden. "The Nomadic Life." *Rita Golden Gelman.com*. http://www.ritagoldengelman.com/the-nomadic-life/. Accessed 16 Jun. 2020.

Gifford, Nancy A. "Kent, Jack. *Joey Runs Away*." *School Library Journal*, vol. 32, Nov. 1985, p. 73.

Glaser, Eleanor. "There's No Such Thing as a Dragon." *School Library Journal*, vol. 22, no. 3, 1975, p. 64.

"Goldsmith, Howard." *International Who's Who of Authors and Writers 2004.* Europa Publications, 2003, p. 209.

"Guessing Who He Is." *Portola Reporter*, 28 Jun 1956, p. 6.

Holland, Steve. "Seymour Reit." *The Guardian*. 23 Dec. 2001. https://www.theguardian.com/news/2001/dec/24/guardianobituaries.books. Accessed 17 Jun. 2020.

"Hollywood Learns the TV Film Craft." *Sponsor*, 10 Mar. 1952, pp. 80–81, 107–10.

References

Holtz, Allan. "Ink-Slinger Profiles: Jack Kent." *Stripper's Guide*. 26 Dec. 2012. http://strippersguide.blospot.com/2012/12/ink-slinger-profiles-jack-kent .html. Accessed 5 Mar. 2020.

"Howard Goldsmith." *Gale Literature: Contemporary Authors*. Gale Literature: Contemporary Authors. 2012. https://link-gale-com.ezproxy.ramsey.lib.mn.us/ apps/doc/H1000037703/CA?u=ramsey_main&sid=CA&xid=1f706b2c. Accessed 17 Apr. 2020.

"Interview: Bruce Canwell on IDW's *King Aroo*." *Westfield Comics Blog*. https:// westfieldcomics.com/blog/interviews-and-columns/interview-bruce-canwell -on-idws-king-aroo/. Accessed 9 Jun. 2020.

"Jack Kent." *Lambiek Comiclopedia*. lambiek.net/artists/k/kent_j.htm. Accessed 14 Mar. 2020.

"John Wellington Kent." *Gale Literature: Contemporary Authors*. Gale in Context: Biography. Document number: GALE H1000053464. 2004.

"John Wellington Kent." 21 Jan. 1985 interview. Gale Literature: Contemporary Authors. 2020. Gale in Context: Biography. Document number: GALE H10800 48707.

Keller, Charles. *Awesome Jokes*. Sterling, 1996.

Kelly, Selby, and Bill Crouch Jr., editors. *The Best of Pogo*. Fireside, 1982.

Kennedy, Karen. "S. A. Illustrator Kent Invited to Decorate White House Egg." *San Antonio Express*, 13 Mar. 1982.

"Kent, Jack." *Fifth Book of Junior Authors and Illustrators*, edited by Sally Holmes Holtze. T. H. Wilson, 1983, pp. 171–73.

Kent, Jack. "What, Why Children Read." *San Antonio Express*, 30 Mar. 1969.

Kent, Jack. "Graphics for Youths." *San Antonio Express*, 27 Sep. 1970.

Kent, Jack. "The Early Bird." *Ladybug*, vol. 9, no. 2, 1998, pp. 26–27.

Kent, Jack. "The Firefly." *Cricket*, vol. 32, no. 11, 2005, p. 4.

Kent, Jack, Jr. "Jack Kent's Home & Work." *Vintage Children's Books My Kid Loves*. 11 Feb. 2010. Available at: http://www.vintagechildrensbooksmykidloves.com/ 2010/02/jack-kents-studio-by-jack-jr.html. Accessed 21 Oct. 2022.

Kent, Jack, Jr. "Jack Kent, King Aroo, and King William." *King William Association*. History—People. 2010. https://www.ourkwa.org/articles/history-people/ 422-jack-kent-king-aroo-and-king-william.

Kent, June. "For Expo—Go!" *San Antonio Express*, 2 Jul. 1967.

Kilstofte, June. "King Aroo's Castle." *San Antonio Express Sunday Magazine*, 1953.

"King Aroo's Creator." *Chicago Tribune*, 12 Oct. 1952.

"King Aroo's Creator Lives on Whimsical Adventures" *Pasadena Independent*, 1 Jul. 1955.

"King Aroo Heir, Long Live Kent!" *Wilmington Daily Press Journal*, 8 Aug. 1955.

Kingman, Lee, Grace Allen Hogarth, and Harriet Quimby. *Illustrators of Children's Books 1967–1976*. Horn Book, 1978.

"Lenahan Outbid for McClure Syndicate." *Wilkes-Barre Times Leader*, 9 Sep. 1952.

Lowman, Al. "The Life and Death of a Bookstore." *Southwestern Historical Quarterly*, vol. 91, no. 2, 1987, pp. 173–84.

M., Jane. "Jack Kent Went from Comic Strips to Children's Books." *Austin American-Statesman*, 31 Aug. 1979.

Maloney, Brenda Durrin. "The Once-Upon-A-Time Dragon." *School Library Journal*, vol. 29, no. 3, 1982, p. 69.

"Marcia McClintock Folsom." *Gale Literature: Contemporary Authors*. 2001. https://link-gale-com.ezproxy.ramsey.lib.mn.us/apps/doc/H1000135630/CA?u=ramsey_main&sid=CA&xid=edc57624. Accessed 17 Apr. 2020.

Marschall, Richard. "God Save the King!" *Nemo: The Classic Comics Library*, no. 21, Aug. 1986, pp. 5–6.

"Mary Elting." *Gale Literature: Contemporary Authors. Gale Literature: Contemporary Authors*. 2001. https://link-gale-com.ezproxy.ramsey.lib.mn.us/apps/doc/H1000029207/CA?u=ramsey_main&sid=CA&xid=a83d49a5. Accessed 17 Apr. 2020.

Mary Elting, Franklin Folsom, and Michael Folsom. "Guide to the Folsom-Elting Collection, 1862–2005, 1930–1995." University of Colorado at Boulder Libraries. https://snaccooperative.org/ark:/99166/w6dw4m1x.

Mecca, Pete. "A Veteran's Story: A Veteran of Zig-Zag Pass." *The Citizens*, 29 Apr. 2018. https://www.rockdalenewtoncitizen.com/features/a-veteran-s-story-a-veteran-of-zig-zag-pass/article_a34f3c87-e335-54b6-985c-a71af95ecae1.html. Accessed 28 Apr. 2020.

"Michael (Brewster) Folsom." *Gale Literature: Contemporary Authors. Gale Literature: Contemporary Authors*. 2003. https://link-gale-com.ezproxy.ramsey.lib.mn.us/apps/doc/H1000032719/CA?u=ramsey_main&sid=CA&xid=17a7153b. Accessed 17 Apr. 2020.

Monypenny, Leslie. "King Aroo's Wit Flows from Pen of Zany Genius." *Chicago Tribune*, 31 Mar. 1952, p. 23.

"New Syndicate Has 'King Aroo.'" *Editor & Publisher*, 19 Mar. 1960.

"Newspaper Promotions Announced." *The Eagle* (Bryan, Texas), 6 Oct. 1969.

North San Antonio Times, 3 Feb. 1977 (Canwell, 2013, p. 18).

"Noted Cartoonist to Be Matrix Dinner Speaker." *San Antonio Express*, 12 Apr. 1959.

Nye, Naomi Shihab. "Rain Falling into the River—That Moment as They Merge." *Mint*. State Street Press Chapbooks, 1991, p. 11.

Oishi, Shigehiro, and Ulrich Schimmak. "Residential Mobility, Well-Being, and Mortality." *Journal of Personality and Social Psychology*, vol. 98, no. 6, 2010, pp. 980–94.

"Outstanding Books of the Year." *New York Times*, 14 Nov. 1976, p. 266.

Palmer, Nancy. "Knee High Nina." *School Library Journal*, vol. 27, no. 7, 1981, p. 133.

"Peter Kilstofte." *The Minneapolis Star*, 29 Jan. 1938.

Phillips, Carol Kolb. "Jim Jimmy James." *School Library Journal*, vol. 30, no. 9, 1984, p. 66.

Pinizzotto, Dana Whitney. "The Scribble Monster." *School Library Journal*, vol. 28, no. 3, 1981, p. 78.

"Polly Berrien Berends." *Gale Literature: Contemporary Authors*. 2001. https://link -gale-com.ezproxy.ramsey.lib.mn.us/apps/doc/H1000007718/CA?u=ramsey_ main&sid=CA&xid=855a4b70. Accessed 17 Apr. 2020.

Ratireri, Steve. "King Aroo." *Library Journal*, vol. 135, no. 12, 2010, p. 66.

"Readers Urged to Re-Register; Inspect New Books at Library." *The Waxahachie Daily Light*, 30 Dec 1969.

Reynolds, Moira Davison. *Comic Strip Artists in American Newspapers 1945–1980*. McFarland, 2015.

"Richard J(ules) Margolis." *Gale Literature: Contemporary Authors*. *Gale Literature: Contemporary Authors*. 2003. https://link-gale.com.ezproxy.ramsey.lib.mn.us/ apps/doc/H1000064016/CA?u=ramsey_main&sid=CA&xid=ba4e57a9. Accessed 17 Apr. 2020.

Roberts, Monte. "Between Times." *Times Colonist* (Victoria, BC), 4 Nov. 1953.

Roberts, Monte. "Between Times." *Times Colonist* (Victoria, BC), 21 Jul. 1955.

Roesch, Roberta Fleming. "Swift Pace Is Needed in Travel Promotion." *Wilkes-Barre Times Leader*, 31 Jan. 1962.

"Royal Comic Strip." *People Today*, 25 Feb. 1953.

"Ruth Belov Gross." *Scholastic.com*. https://www.scholastic.com/teachers/authors/ ruth--belov-gross/. Accessed 18 Apr. 2020.

Santos, John Phillip. "City of Dreams." *Texas Monthly*, Jun. 2010.

Sawyer, Eve Lynn. "Flotsam and Jet Some." *San Antonio Express and News*, 11 May 1969.

Sawyer, Eve Lynn. "Educational Tour Turns to Pleasure Trip." *San Antonio Express and News*, 27 Nov. 1974.

Seldes, Gilbert. "Introduction." *King Aroo*. Doubleday, 1953, pp. 5–8.

Shannon, Patrick. "Hidden within the Pages: A Study of Social Perspective in Young Children's Favorite Books." *The Reading Teacher*, vol. 39, no. 7, 1986, pp. 656–63.

Smith, Ruth. "Wonderful Land of Make Believe Is the Scene." *Orlando Sentinel*, 22 Mar. 1953.

"St. Luke's School Book Fair to Have Jack Kent as Guest." *San Antonio Express*, 21 Oct. 1970.

Streetman, Burgin. "Just Only Jack." *San Antonio Current*, 10 Feb. 2010.

Tisserand, Michael. *Krazy: George Herriman, A Life in Black and White*. Harpe, 2016, p. 410.

References 171

"Tresselt, Alvin." *Twentieth Century Children's Writers*, edited by D. L. Kirkpatrick. Macmillan, 1978, p. 1251.

Walker, Brian. *The Comics: The Complete Collection*. Abrams, 2004.

"Well-Known Author/Illustrators to Speak." *Hartford Courant,* 7 May 1978.

Wepman, Dennis. "Kent, John Wellington (Jack Kent)." *Contemporary Graphic Artists*, vol. 1, edited by Maurice Horn. Gale Research Company. 1986, pp. 159–62.

White, Ron. "Chasing a Child's Summer Boredom." *San Antonio Express*, 6 Aug. 1972.

White, Ron. "Jack Kent: Just a Kid at Heart." *San Antonio Express Sunday Magazine*, 23 Jun. 1974.

Williams, Barbara. "Little Heroine Too Helpful." *San Antonio Express*, 9 Mar. 1969.

Williams, Barbara. "Elephants Do, Too, Forget." *San Antonio Express*, 30 Mar. 1969, p. 104.

Williams, Barbara. "Charming New Story for Children." *San Antonio Express*, 20 Apr. 1969.

World Encyclopedia of Comics, The. Edited by Maurice Horn. Chelsea House, 1976.

"World War II in Alaska." *National Park Service*, 20 Jan. 2016. nps.gov/articles/world-war-ii-in-alaska.htm. Accessed 28 Apr. 2020.

"Young Book World." *Austin American-Statesman*, 6 Apr. 1975.

Index

Aesop, 51, 76, 80, 92, 94, 111, 147
Aleutian Islands, 17–19
Allen, Leigh, 30–31, 34, 38
Animobile Book, The, 110, 144
Antiques Roadshow, 142
Arnold, George Stanleigh, 53, 54, 57, 63, 136
Arriola, Gus, 68, 69

Barchas, Sarah E., 100, 104, 150
Berends, Polly Berrien, 86, 149
Big Bear, Spare That Tree!, 107, 153
Big Chief Wahoo, 16, 22
Biggest Shadow in the Zoo, The, 126
Bishop, Bonnie, 104, 152
Blah, The, 84–85, 102, 115, 125, 136
Boyette, Pat, 46
Bremen Town Musicians, The, 99, 149
Bridgman, Juliet, 34–40, 44, 47
Burlington, Iowa, 3, 4, 9

Caldecott Medal, 79, 153
Caniff, Milton, 13
Canwell, Bruce, 136, 138–39
Carroll, Lewis, 28, 42–43, 48, 77
CBS (TV station), 35, 37, 153
Christmas Piñata, The, 115–16
Cindy Lou and the Witch's Dog, 105–6, 115, 133–34
Clotilda, 80–82, 86, 102, 114, 121, 140, 147
Collier's Weekly, 9–10, 73

Congoleum Company, 4, 10
Cummins, Kent, 19, 59, 77, 132–33, 148
Cummins, Mary Lou, 4–9, 19–20, 85, 128–29

de Regniers, Beatrice Shenk. *See* Regniers, Beatrice Shenk de
Dooly and the Snortsnoot, 93, 116, 147–48

Easy as Pie, 124, 154
Egg Book, The, 101, 113
Elting, Mary, 154
Emperor's New Clothes, The, 104, 147

Far Side, The, 136
Fat Cat, The, 90–92, 114, 133, 146–47
Ferguson Map Company, 55, 63, 67, 82, 86
Floyd, the Tiniest Elephant, 114, 148
Fly Away Home, 80–81, 127
Folsom, Marcia, 155
Folsom, Michael, 124, 154–55
Fox and the Crow, The. *See* Aesop
Funny Book, The, 105

Gelman, Rita Golden, 104, 151
Girl Who Wouldn't Get Married, The, 109, 146
Goldberg, Rube, 14, 25, 27
Goldsmith, Howard, 124, 155
Great Depression, 10, 44

Index

Greenwillow Press, 107, 113, 124, 145
Grime Doesn't Pay: Law and Order Jokes, 124, 153–54
Gross, Ruth Belov, 99, 104, 108–9, 149
Grown-Up Day, The, 83–84, 86, 125, 129
Gruelle, Johnny, 77

Herriman, George, 8, 15, 17–18, 27, 39, 41, 55, 63, 73
Hirschman, Susan, 101, 107, 113, 124–25
Hoddy Doddy, 107
How Did They Get from Here to There When George Washington Was Young?, 108–9
How to Make Possum's Honey Bread, 100, 149–50
Humpty Dumpty's Magazine for Little Children, 69–70, 73, 78, 94–95, 111, 113–14, 156–57

I Was Walking Down the Road, 100, 104–5, 133, 146, 148, 150
IDW Publishing, 138, 155
If You Grew Up with George Washington, 108, 149

Jack Kent's Book of Fables, 92–94, 147
Jack Kent's Book of Nursery Tales, 86, 90, 106, 147, 149
Jack Kent's Happy Ever After Book, 106, 113–14
Jack Kent's Hocus Pocus Bedtime Book, 106, 148
Jack Kent's Hop, Skip and Jump Book, 101, 130, 146, 148
Jack Kent's Merry Mother Goose, 105, 114, 132, 148
Jack Kent's Twelve Days of Christmas, 96–97
Jack Kent's Valentines Sticker Book, 110
Janie and the Giant, 104, 150

Jim Jimmy James, 124–26, 147
Joey, 125–26, 146, 148
Joey Runs Away, 126–27, 132, 146–47
Johnson, Crockett, 20, 77, 137
Just Only John, 77–80, 87, 89, 116, 134

Keller, Charles, 124, 153–54
Kelly, Walt, 23, 24, 26–27, 29, 49, 77
Kent, Jack: Army career of, 17–21, 36, 59, 111; childhood of, 3–11, 36, 77, 127; death of, 128; education of, 4–10, 14–15, 19, 111–12; political views of, 59–61; religious views of, 119–21
Kent, Jack, Jr., 47–48, 60, 63, 67–72, 76–77, 80–82, 95, 108, 113–14, 119–20, 125, 128, 130, 132, 135, 140–42
Kent, June, 43–47, 54–56, 60–61, 67–69, 81–82, 86, 90, 95, 98–99, 118–19, 121–22, 127–30, 133, 139–41, 148
Kent, Mary Lou. *See* Cummins, Mary Lou
Kent, Peg, 3–7, 9, 19, 30, 44, 47, 55, 124, 127
Kent, Ralph, 3–7, 9–11, 13, 19, 22, 30, 47, 54, 114, 127
King Aroo: allusions in, 50–52; influence on children's books, 80–81, 89, 92–94, 96–97, 102, 105–6, 114–16, 125–27, 136; influences of, 26–28, 42–43; influences on comic strips, 134–36; visual style of, 24, 26, 49, 53–54; wordplay in, 32–33, 134–35
Knee-High Nina, 116, 125, 148
Krazy Kat. *See* Herriman, George
Kuekes, Edward D., 56

Laura's Story, 104, 153
L'il Abner, 14, 135–36

174 Index

Little Annie Rooney, 9
Little Church Around the Corner, 36
Little Peep, 126, 133, 146
Littledale, Freya, 103–4, 151

Mad Magazine, 72–73, 84, 114, 138, 151–52, 156
Magic Carrot Seeds, The, 149–50
Margolis, Richard J., 107, 153
McClure Newspaper Syndicate, 24–26, 36, 40, 52, 138
McNamara, Tom, 9, 13
Minnesota Farmer–Labor Party, 60
More Fables of Aesop, 92–93
More Spaghetti, I Say, 104, 151
Mr. Elephant's Birthday Party, 80–81, 96
Mr. Meebles, 85–86, 94, 102, 121, 146
Mrs. Mooley, 96–97, 101, 132, 146–48

New Yorker, 13, 73, 76
No One Noticed Ralph, 104, 152
Nye, Naomi Shihab, 121–24, 129, 139–42

Once-Upon-a-Time Dragon, The, 116–17, 123

Parents' Magazine Press, 78–79, 83–85, 92, 97, 104, 115, 133, 151
Peanuts, 25, 39–41, 54, 69, 135
Piggy Bank Gonzales, 127
Playboy, 69, 72, 155–56
Pogo. See Kelly, Walt

Q Is for Duck, 124, 154

Ralph Rides Away, 104, 152
Regniers, Beatrice Schenk de, 104, 153
Rice University, 9, 95, 108
Ringling Brothers and Barnum and Bailey Circus, 34–35, 38

Rosengren, Camille, 38, 129, 148
Rosengren's Books, 14–16, 97–98, 118, 148
Round Robin, 110, 114–15, 133, 146
Ruben Award, 41

San Antonio Express and News, 43–47, 55, 68–69, 82, 95, 121–22
San Antonio Light, 10, 12–13, 77
Saturday Evening Post, 35, 72, 133, 156
Scholastic, 95, 100, 103, 108–10, 144–45, 147–48
Scribble Monster, The, 114, 132–33, 145
Seger, E. C., 9
Seldes, Gilbert, 39–41, 61
Sendak, Maurice, 136, 153
Seven at One Blow, 104
Silly Goose, 111–12, 124
Simple Prince, The, 104, 152
Socks for Supper, 106, 132
Spanish Governor's Palace (San Antonio), 29
St. Mark's Episcopal Church, 119, 121, 129
Steig, William, 10, 11, 77, 97
Stevens, Carla, 100, 149–50
Supermarket Magic: A Sniffy Book, 114, 133

Tagalog language, 20, 33
There's No Such Thing as a Dragon, 101–2, 132–33, 147–48
Tiny and Tony: A Golden Book of Picture Postcards, 104, 146
Tobey, Barney, 10, 69, 89
Tresselt, Alvin, 78–79, 86
Twiddle Twins' Haunted House, The, 120, 155

University of Minnesota, 45, 130, 139, 153

White House Easter Egg Roll, 110
Why Can't I Fly?, 104, 148, 151
"Why Christmas Almost Wasn't,"
    73–75
Wizard and His Magic Spells, The. See
    Wizard of Wallaby Wallow, The
Wizard of Id, The, 136
Wizard of Wallaby Wallow, The, 89, 102,
    116, 132, 146–48
Woggon, Elmer. See *Big Chief Wahoo*
Women Flyers, 45
World War II, 17–21

Yolen, Jane, 104, 152

Zurawski, John, 3, 5
Zurawski, Rudolph. *See* Kent, Ralph

About the Author

Photo courtesy of the author

Paul V. Allen is author and researcher with a special interest in the lives and work of creative people. His books include *Eleanor Cameron: Dimensions of Amazement* and *I Can Read It All by Myself: The Beginner Books Story*, both published by University Press of Mississippi. He lives in Normal, Illinois.

CPSIA information can be obtained
at www.ICGtesting.com
Printed in the USA
JSHW082155290623
43591JS00001B/6

9 781496 846280